The Kentigern Way

A life and Lakeland pilgrimage

Also by Stephen G Wright:

Coming Home – Notes for the Journey
Guidance on the principles of spiritual awakening.

Contemplation
An exploration of the contemplative Way down the ages with suggestions for opening to the experience.

Beloved
A poem of mystical union.

Burnout
A self help guide

Yours, Faithfully
Poetic reflections on conversations with the Beloved.

Sacred Space: Right Relationship and Spirituality in Healthcare
(with Jean Sayre-Adams)

All from Sacred Space Publications, Penrith
also at www.sacredspace.org.uk

'God for All' in Cumbria and the Sacred Space Foundation support the Kentigern School for contemplatives. For more information contact richard.passmore@carlislediocese.org.uk

THE KENTIGERN WAY

A life and Lakeland pilgrimage

Stephen G Wright

wild goose publications

www.ionabooks.com

First published 2019

Wild Goose Publications
21 Carlton Court, Glasgow G5 9JP, UK
www.ionabooks.com
Wild Goose Publications is the publishing division of the Iona Community.
Scottish Charity No. SC003794. Limited Company Reg. No. SC096243.

ISBN 978-1-84952-702-6
Cover photograph © William James

Overseas distribution:
Australia: Willow Connection Pty Ltd, Unit 4A, 3-9 Kenneth Road, Manly Vale, NSW 2093
New Zealand: Pleroma, Higginson Street, Otane 4170, Central Hawkes Bay
Canada: Novalis/Bayard Publishing & Distribution, 10 Lower Spadina Ave., Suite 400, Toronto, Ontario M5V 2Z2

Printed by Bell & Bain, Thornliebank, Glasgow

CONTENTS

FOREWORD

Kentigern is probably the closest Cumbria comes to having a 'patron saint'. In the 6th and early 7th centuries he re-evangelised much of the area and had a particular association with Crosthwaite (Keswick) where he preached to a large gathering and erected a cross. Stephen Wright's fascination with his colourful subject shines through this account of Kentigern's life, which emphasises his compassion, ministry and prayerfulness, and punctures the bubble of medieval hagiography. Kentigern's relevance for today is located firmly in his 'struggle to make sense of the world and live fully in it, and to help others do likewise' during a very difficult and troubled time. He comes across as an attractive character whose passion for sharing his deep Christian faith and ability to 'draw people along the way' has plenty of resonance today.

But this delightfully accessible book isn't just a biography. No less than nine churches in Cumbria have a close association with Kentigern, and Stephen Wright has put together a ninety-mile pilgrimage, which involves walking between and visiting them all. He explores the difference between being a 'tourist' and a 'pilgrim' (which is essentially the consciousness with which we travel) and helpfully observes that 'it is not so much that we take a pilgrimage – but rather that pilgrimage takes us'. 'Pilgrimage,' he says, 'is a time when you can open yourself fully to the Beloved.' It is 'slow religion' (like slow food or slow radio) which allows us to 'step aside from the normal rhythm of life for a while and listen more deeply to that still small voice within'.

Along the way he provides both practical advice and spiritual guidance, with pertinent questions to ask oneself at each stage of the journey. Reflecting on where we have been, where we are, and where we are going is something we all need to do, and this book relates directly to the widespread desire in our frenetic culture for a meaningful spirituality.

So this little book hits several targets.

Historians will enjoy the honest assessment of Kentigern's life and some revealing asides about the reality of Celtic culture. Walkers will find an enthralling travel guide and a beautiful, manageable route. Contemplatives will be encouraged by the emphasis on listening and stillness. And I challenge anyone not to be inspired and intrigued by the thoughtfulness and love that have gone into researching and producing this unusual and compelling work.

James Newcome
Bishop of Carlisle

Preface

Kentigern is the English name for a saint who, if the stories about him are true, was born in what is now Scotland in the early decades of the 6th century and died in the opening years of the 7th. He was baptised by a man who became his mentor and father-figure, Saint Serf (Latin *Servanus*), the abbot of a monastery at Culross on the north shore of the Firth of Forth. His name in the Brythonic language of the time is variously written as *Cyndyern, Cyndeyrn, Cunderyn, Cunotigernos, Conthigirn, Kyentyern* and in Latin as *Kentigernus*. It is believed to be rooted in two Brythonic words, *cyn* (hound) and *tigerno* (lord or chief), but he is also known, especially in Scotland, by the familiar name of Mungo, a 'pet' name from the Brythonic *mun ghu, minghu* or *fynghu* meaning 'little darling' or 'my dear one' – the kind of words anyone might use on seeing a newborn baby and which Serf is said to have exclaimed at first sight of him. Jocelin, a monk from Furness writing in the 12th century, has Serf uttering the same words in Irish Gaelic – '*mochoche*'. The latter provides the root of the name of the parish of Kirkmahoe in Dumfriesshire; otherwise many churches and parishes, especially in Scotland, Wales and Northern England, use Kentigern or Mungo. For simplicity and continuity in this text (not least because St Kentigern's is the name of the church in the village where I live and where the pilgrimage in Part 2 begins) I have used Kentigern throughout.

I came to live in Cumbria almost 25 years ago, fulfilling a lifetime's hope, and ended up in the lovely Mungrisdale (Mungo's valley). My participation in the life of our small church came a little later, yet I could not help but be intrigued by the Kentigern–Mungo name all around me. What kind of man was he to leave such a legacy? What form did his Christianity take? Is he relevant to contemporary spirituality? Did he even exist at all?

Nothing written by Kentigern himself has survived. If he had a story to tell it is invisible to us. Only in local legends, hand-me-down tales and place names are there hints of the man he was. Jocelin, a monk of Furness in what is now Cumbria, describes in his *Vita* (Life) his version of Kentigern but, as we shall see, this account is highly suspect. Beyond this we can only guess what Kentigern taught and the way he taught. This is risky, for we can easily project our own agenda onto him or see him as a righteous proponent of Roman Catholicism (as seems to be Jocelin's intent).

As the years passed I delved more and more into the stories about him and visited places associated with his life. History is not always helpful in getting to know the person; initially Kentigern seemed like one of those 'stuffed specimens' of the saints that Evelyn Underhill describes, 'exhibited against a flat tapestried background, more or less picturesque, but always thought of in opposition to the concrete thickness of the modern world'. I found that walking in his footsteps was not a bad way to get free of the 'stuffed specimen', discover the man and illuminate his relevance for today. Later I set about creating a pilgrimage connecting the churches that form a circular route around the glorious northern fells of Cumbria. What follows are some answers to questions about the reality or otherwise of Kentigern, along with a description of the route of the pilgrimage and its impact.

ACKNOWLEDGEMENTS

I am grateful to:

- Jeannie Sayre-Adams, Kristopher Drummond and William James for their help with editing and proof-reading (and to William for the cover photo). My special appreciation goes to Sandra Kramer and Neil Paynter at Wild Goose for all the work in getting this book into print, and to Jane Riley for her wonderful artwork.
- St Mungo's Cathedral, Glasgow, especially the librarian and archivist Iain MacNair, for access to writings about Kentigern and especially the facsimile of Jocelin's *Vita*.
- The Iona Community for access to the Abbey library containing many old, rare and undated texts that include accounts of Kentigern.
- Marsh's Library in Dublin for access to the original *Vita*.
- Jim Johnson for providing access to the closed St Kentigern Church in Grinsdale.
- Elizabeth Reed, Churchwarden, for information on St Giles' Church, Great Orton.
- Bishop James Newcome for his enthusiasm and support for this project.
- Lesley Orr for her insights and willingness to contribute Teneu's perspective.

PART 1

KENTIGERN – HIS TIME AND PLACE: A BACKGROUND

Was he real?

It's possible that Kentigern as a specifically identified individual did not exist. The few contemporary written sources we have about his time (the 6th century) do not mention him and what we do have is derived from much later medieval documents of dubious origin.

Many accounts of Kentigern's life have been produced (for example Glass, Hale, Keelivine, Leatham, Macdonald), invariably and uncritically following that set out in the *Vita* written by Jocelin of Furness in the 12th century. Macquarrie offers a more circumspect approach regarding the 'obscure figure' that is Kentigern and illuminates the difficulty of relying on the account of Jocelin. The latter was engaged in 'stitching together' Kentigern's story some six hundred years after his death and, having an agenda to pursue in doing so, has made the discernment of the truth of Kentigern's life much more difficult. Written records surviving from Kentigern's time are few and far between. The post-Roman period in Britain was a time of confusion, conflict, disease and piracy, and new cultures were emerging, forged from the remnants of Roman influence, the tribalism of indigenous Britons and the impact of migrants.

Added to the mix was the gradual establishment in lands west of the Clyde (in modern-day Argyll, the Western Isles and southwest Scotland) of an Irish Gaelic kingdom: *Dal Riada* (from Gaelic *dal* meaning portion or territory and *Riata*, probably a tribal or chieftain's name). The Scotii/Scoti was the name given by the Romans to these Gaelic-Irish raiders (for booty and slaves) of the west coast of their British province, *Britannia*. They eventually gave their name and language to what was to become Scotland. The Scotii also enter the edges of this story as captors and enslavers of Patrick, son a of a Romanised north-Briton and probably the most famous of all the early British saints. He took with him to Ireland in the 5th century the British form of Christianity – a lineage that was to affect not only Ireland but also the development of Christianity along the western seaboard of Britannia and beyond, not least through later followers and pilgrim monks such as Columba.

Lastly, to add to the stew of conflict in Kentigern's time, waves of colonisers were arriving from mainland Europe. These Germanic peoples – Saxons, Angles, Frisians and Jutes – brought with them their Pagan beliefs and their different ways of seeing the world and organising society. Further north and west, the indigenous Pictish tribes also vied for power and territory.

Somehow, from within the fog of truth and conjecture about this volatile time, the Kentigern story emerges. While some have questioned his very existence, others (Gough-Cooper) have suggested a case of confused identity with a Gaulish bishop of similar name from Paris. Still others believe that he was a conflation of several heroic and religious persons embellished by hopes and storytelling in a time of conflict – a kind of Christian, Brythonic Robin Hood. Kentigern may thus be a 'composite figure, groomed if not born in the imagination of his hagiographer' which, argues Lynch, comes 'at the expense of the trials of successive generations of missionaries whose role remains obscure and unsung'.

Although many of the later accounts of Kentigern's life are rooted in stories handed down in oral tradition, it is too easy to dismiss them for that reason. It seems that there is enough evidence, not least place names, ancient documents (such as the *Annales Cambriae*) and long-held traditions, that help us to be reasonably sure that Kentigern was, in the words of Macquarrie, 'a real historical figure'.

Kentigern's story in Jocelin's hagiography does indeed make for fascinating reading, being full of miraculous events, grand vistas of history and intriguing plot lines. The veracity of much of Jocelin's account is questionable, although many have chosen down the years to accept it at face value. However, the inclination to deny the facts in preference of a good fantasy need not detract from the reality of Kentigern as a living, breathing person. We can be reasonably certain that he walked the earth sometime between 520 and 615 AD and that he was sufficiently influential to impress himself on the lives and memories of those he encountered.

Kentigern's Britannia – from Roman to post-Roman

In the year 518 AD, Britannia was in trouble. Indeed it had been for over 150 years. Raiders, migrants, mercenaries and colonisers – Pictish peoples largely from north of the Antonine Wall, Irish pirates and slavers, and Angles and Saxons from across the North Sea – were hastening the disintegration of Roman authority, already exacerbated by internal power struggles and fragile alliances among the Romano-British peoples.

In the hope of peace and stability, in the early years of the 5th century, some Romanised Britons had backed a pretender, Flavius Claudius Constantinus – a common soldier of some military skill – for the imperial Roman throne in the face of the incumbent Honorius. The Romano-British authorities feared the invasion of Germanic tribes that were sweeping all before them in mainland Europe and invested their security in Constantinus, who was briefly to become co-emperor as Constantine III. Power struggles in the Western

Roman Empire continued as a divided empire lost its centralised authority across vast swathes of what had hitherto been Roman territory.

That loss of authority had gone on for many decades in Britannia, leading to a gradual breakdown of control, commerce and collective civic responsibility in British towns and provinces. Indeed, the original Roman method of governance may have contributed to it. The inclination was to develop the *civitas* (pl. *civitates*), the city-state, as a central unit of government in conquered lands. London, York, Chester and Carlisle (one of the largest), for example, later emerged as city-states ready to fill at least part of the vacuum created by the eventual withdrawal of imperial Roman power.

Meanwhile, early Britannia had little in the way of cities or towns and the *civitas*, according to historian Stuart Laycock, was at first gradually invested in trusted local tribes, or perhaps more accurately in their aristocracy. The image of Romans invading and putting their own people in charge wears thin under these circumstances. Roman conquest invariably meant that at least some of the old bosses became the new bosses, exchanging their halls of wood, wattle and daub for more luxurious villas. It is not difficult to imagine how, in times of conflict, this method of government might revert to isolationism and independent action.

However, backing Constantinus in 408 AD seems to have made matters worse. From his British base he crossed the channel to assert his emperorship, presumably taking with him a large part of the available troops. Faced with relentless internal struggles, treachery and invasions from many quarters, Honorius gave way and made Constantinus joint consul, but it was not to last long. Defeated at Arles, Constantinus was executed while a prisoner en route to Ravenna in about 411. He was the last agent of centralised Roman power in Britannia.

Meanwhile, the security situation within Britannia worsened. Central authority continued to be eroded as people turned to trusting local leaders or went off-grid and avoided civic involvement, including paying taxes, while defences weakened and encroachments from invaders worsened. Having backed the wrong horse in Constantinus, the Britons' appeals to Rome and Emperor Honorius for help fell on deaf ears and he famously told them to 'look to their own defences'.

In any case he was in no position to help. The Western Roman Empire was beleaguered by external attacks and internal turmoil. The Visigoths sacked Rome in 410 AD. It had long since ceased to be the capital of the empire; in the east this had been ceded to the 'New Rome' – Byzantium/Constantinople – and in the west to *Mediolanum* (Milan) in 286 and Ravenna in 402. Yet the capture of Rome, the historic, economic, political and spiritual centre of the empire for a thousand years, sent shock waves across the continent.

Urban life, what there was of it, and the connectedness of the various *civitates* in Britannia continued their decline. Without a centralising authority, the *Pax Romana* began to dissolve as civic government, administration and rule of law dissipated and devolved to whoever could grab the most power or was willing to take on the responsibility thrust on them by local communities. Imperial coinage had ceased to be delivered to Britannia fifty years before. While local warlords and other leaders sought to assert their authority, old tribal and familial loyalties began to re-emerge as a dominant force – the pattern of governance known to the British peoples before the Roman conquest.

Another cause of disorder was a new sickness. Justinian's plague, occurring during the reign of the Eastern Roman emperor Justinian, is the first recorded evidence of a global pandemic. Originating in China and passing along trade routes, this early form of bubonic plague devastated human populations, with deaths estimated between 25 and 50 million people. Some historians, such as Wacher, suggest the impact on Britannia was to weaken the defence forces of the Romano-British population. Plague hit the country more readily because of the extensive continental and Mediterranean trading links and the indigenous population's inclination to live in small rural groups rather than towns, cities and garrison communities. Whatever the case, in these early years of Kentigern's life, around 550 AD, if plague was decimating centres of population held by the *civitates*, then this would advantage the opposition. The Anglo-Saxon colonisation, held in check after the legendary battle at Badon Hill around 500 AD, seems to have been reinvigorated. Renewed strife, land-grabbing, reversion to Paganism and increased danger in travel was evident in Kentigern's time.

Such conflict and economic collapse can produce huge movements of peoples as some head for the nearest place of safety as refugees or occupy land and settlements abandoned by others. For example, some Britons, perhaps the better off, escaped to their kin in what was to become Brittany in northern France. It is a familiar pattern in times of conflict that those with the wealth or connections or the nous to see what is coming are best placed to escape. However, the historical evidence does not suggest wholesale chaos. Battles and power struggles between local warlords and elites do not seem to have affected everyone. Settlers were often integrated rather than fought and, for some people at least, times of strife alternated with times of relative peace. If this were not so, the continued expansion of the Christian church and its institutions could not have occurred.

Nevertheless, Britannia had essentially become, as Laycock suggests, a 'failed state'. By the time of Kentigern's birth, central Roman governance was over. Some local leaders sought to maintain a Romano-British inheritance; others broke away to establish their own over-lordship. Modern equivalents would be Yugoslavia in the late 20th century and Libya or Syria in the early years of the 21st. Once the power at the centre holding things together is emptied out, all manner of competing interests assert themselves to fill the vacuum.

This was the beginning of the 'Dark Ages' – dark not because they were times of particular evil, but because we know so little about them. The decline of Roman authority took with it many aspects of Roman culture including the keeping of written records. Just as tribal patterns of governance re-emerged, so we are left with only hand-me-down oral accounts of events. The oral tradition before the Roman invasion was the primary way of passing on history, as it still is among non-literate peoples today. We tend to regard these accounts as questionable. To what extent are these stories mere fabrication, essential truth or a mixture of both?

During this 'Dark Age', as Roman supremacy declined, new stories and mythologies arose to give people a sense of meaning, purpose and rootedness in their lives. About this time we see the birth of an archetypical British mythology – that of Arthur. It is also the age of Kentigern. The lives of these two heroic figures have many common threads. Both were men of their time, deeply influenced by the history and culture that had formed them and those around them. They were not beamed down as ready-made heroes disconnected from the values, customs and worldviews of the Romanised life that preceded them.

The Roman Empire in Britannia had extended up to central Scotland on the banks of the Tay, eventually pulling back to the modern-day Scottish Lowlands. The Antonine Wall, commissioned by Emperor Antonius Pius (about 142 AD), became a border for defence, taxation and trade stretching from the Firth of Forth in the east to the Clyde in the west. Built mainly of turf, on stone foundations and with wooden ramparts, it provided a marker for Roman authority, only to be largely abandoned about ten years later in favour of the stronger, more southerly boundary of Hadrian's Wall (begun in 122 AD), which stretched from the Tyne estuary in the east to the Solway Firth in the west. The territory between the two walls became a buffer zone. If the Antonine Wall was the first line of defence, then Hadrian's was to be the red line held against all comers.

Just as the lands south of Hadrian's Wall later had to learn to adjust to the decline of Roman rule, so those in this buffer zone must have adapted to being a halfway house. Local tribal elites held on to their authority and traditions or perhaps created mergers of the Roman and the British ways of life. Being neither quite one nor the other, they forged alliances and governance as it suited them, simply using 'what works'. It is in this zone, from the cloudy waters of mystery, myth, legend and oral history, that the story of Kentigern begins to surface.

Although, or perhaps because, accurate historical records for this 'Dark Age' are scant, the Arthurian legend emerges during this same period. A picture forms of a charismatic, valiant Romano-British leader who rallied the tribes and the *civitates* sufficiently to stem the Anglo-Saxon incursions in the 6th century. His heroic exploits covered large parts of what is now southern Scotland and down along the northeast and west of England into Wales, Devon and Cornwall. The mysterious figure that is Arthur, made thus by layers of legend, fantasy and projection down the centuries, became everybody's hero. He may have been a real person or a composite of many heroic leaders. He may have been an exceptionally gifted individual or the invention of a people desperate for leadership, hope and peace. Various parts of the country have laid claim to him. Historian Michael Wood inclines to the existence of a northern Romano-British leader, based probably around the *civitas* of Carlisle, sufficiently gifted to inspire and unite the fractious Britons. His exploits and successes in war were enough to capture the imagination and survive in folk memory. The details of Arthur's story are bound up with the origins and ministry of his near contemporary, Kentigern.

Despite the tribalism, there was sufficient common ground of language and culture from present-day southern Scotland down through the north and west of England and further south that, as Nora Chadwick has asserted, 'a traveller could have set off from Edinburgh, and walked through Cumberland, and along the Welsh Border to Land's End, and he would have had no difficulty in making himself understood all the way.'

Kentigern's life in the 6th and the early years of the 7th centuries places him squarely in times of trouble and transition for Britannia. It is here, in the tribe known to the Romans as the *Votadini* and to themselves as the *Gododdin*, that his story arises. His later mission seems to have taken place mainly amongst those peoples with whom he would presumably have no difficulty in making himself understood, peoples to whom kinship and hospitality were important values. Here he stood a good chance of finding welcome and refuge. Here allegiances also crossed boundaries, such as the relationship between the kingdoms of Rheged and Strathclyde that perhaps helped acceptance of him as he worked across them.

Of language and country

The English word Britain is derived from the writings of early Greek explorers and writers such as Pytheas, Diodorus and Strabo. The Greek word *Prettanike* evolved later into *Brettaniai* and *Britannia* among the Romans. The Roman province of Britannia was the island comprising modern-day Scotland, Wales and England, although Roman governance largely came to a halt at the Antonine Wall. The most likely origin is the name that Pytheas suggests the inhabitants had for themselves – *Pretani*, 'painted ones', which seems to refer to their habit of abundant use of body paint and tattoos. Earlier classical texts also refer to the whole of the British Isles as Albion, a term which later came to be applied only to that part which was to become Scotland – *Alba*. Its origins are obscure, perhaps derived from an early British word meaning 'islands', 'land', 'world' or 'region' or possibly from the Latin *albus* (white) – a reference to the white cliffs of the south coast of England.

The language spoken on this collection of islands, before the Roman period, probably evolved along with variations in culture from an original common Brythonic tongue. By the time of the arrival of the Romans, Ireland, never part of the empire, had developed its own distinctive form of Irish Gaelic. The Pictish peoples of the north and west of the island of Britannia spoke a Brythonic language different from the many regional variations and tribal groupings further south. Their lands were mainly north of the Antonine Wall but they also seem to have held territories south of what is now Glasgow and in Ayrshire and Galloway. The Picts, whose origins and culture remain mysterious, appear to have been so named from the Latin *Pictii*, meaning 'painted ones'. Others, such as Stuart McHardy, have reappraised the assumptions of Pictish history suggesting they may have been one of the earliest Neolithic groups to emerge in Britain and may have taken their name from a misunderstanding of the word *pecht* meaning 'ancestor peoples'.

Echoes of the early Brythonic tongues are found in Breton (in northwest France), Cornish and Welsh. Together with Scottish, Irish and Manx Gaelic they are nowadays collectively described as 'Celtic' languages. However, they have so diverged down the centuries that 'Celtic' speakers from these different groups have little in common linguistically and struggle to understand each other.

Yet, in the 6th century, as Nora Chadwick has argued, there were sufficient commonalities of language in lowland Scotland and Western England for Kentigern to have travelled and made himself understood. Indeed, if the birth and childhood accounts by Jocelin are accurate, his origins take in the area now known as the Lothians in south eastern Scotland and the area north of the Firth of Forth around Culross. It is likely he could have spoken both the Brythonic language of his tribe the *Votadini/Gododdin* and Pictish, whose people were also occupying neighbouring lands and often mingled with the *Votadini*. In *Dal Riada*, the *Scotii* were introducing their own Irish Gaelic, but Kenitgern's knowledge of this language would seem to have been more limited as indicated in stories in the *Vita*. If his education in the monastery of St Serf/Servanus at Culross is accurate, then he must also have mastered Latin – the language of the elite and of the church – and possibly Greek.

However, for the vast majority of ordinary people Latin or Greek would have been incomprehensible and very few could read or write. Then, and for centuries to come, Latin remained the language of Christianity throughout Western Europe as part of the mystery and mysticism of the faith. Missionaries like Kentigern needed a command of Latin for priestly duties, but to reach out to the common people they had to speak the common tongues. Thus it is not surprising that most of the stories of Kentigern come from Wales, Cumbria, central and southern Scotland, north east England and as far north into Pictish lands as Aberdeen. Kentigern, and the faith he carried, could be more easily remembered and embraced because he spoke the language of ordinary people.

That language has echoes down the centuries in place names. The *Votadini* had their headquarters around the ancient sacred and administrative site of Traprain Law (probably Brythonic *tref,* 'farm' or 'settlement', and *pren*, 'tree' or 'wooden', or *bryn*, 'hill', and Old English *hlaw*, 'burial mound'). It is found on old maps as Dunpendrylaw, Dounprenderlaw, Dunprender or Dumpender and is locally still known as Dunpelder – possibly derived from the Brythonic *dun*, 'fort', and *pelydr*, 'spear shafts'. Later, likely within Kentigern's lifetime and under pressure from Anglo-Saxon incursions, Traprain Law was abandoned in favour of a (presumably better) defensive site that was to become, in English, Edinburgh (from Scottish Gaelic *aodann,* 'rock face', and Old English *burh*, 'stronghold').

Traprain Law is a natural defensive site, rising above the undulating coastal plain of the Lothians between Edinburgh and Dunbar. Viewed from the north and south it lies like the body of a great beached whale, rising some 221 metres above sea level and surrounded by rich farmland, with the deep gash of a disused quarry on its northern side and a sheer drop to the south. It was here, or very close by, that Kentigern was conceived, but it was not to be the place of his birth. It is not known if he ever returned here. Perhaps its abandonment in favour of Edinburgh and the dangers associated with Pagan incursions would have made it inaccessible to him, even if he had wanted to go back.

Many other place names bear witness to the early Brythonic inhabitants of southern Scotland, some of which have a part to play in the Kentigern story, for example:

- Aberlady (Brythonic/Pictish *aber,* 'river mouth' and Old English 'lady')
- Dumbarton ('stronghold of the Britons', from the Scottish Gaelic *dun*, 'fortified stronghold', and *Breatainn*, 'of the Britons')

- Dunragit (Scottish Gaelic, 'fort of *Rheged*'. Rheged was one of the Brythonic kingdoms of the *Hen Ogledd* – the 'Old North') and was at various times independent, or governed by or a client of the kingdom of Strathclyde. At its zenith it appeared to extend into modern Dumfries and Galloway, and even into southern Lancashire and south-western Yorkshire)
- Glasgow (Brythonic *glas*, 'green place', and *cau*, 'hollow'), although some sources suggest the name may be a derivative mixture of Brythonic *eglas*, 'family/community/church', and *cu* or *ghu*, 'dear/beloved'
- Lanark (Brythonic *llanerc*, 'forest glade').

Further south the names in the landscape are also redolent of the early Brythonic-speaking inhabitants, not least in the county of Cumbria, whence this book originates:

- Carlisle (Brythonic *Caer Luel*; *caer*, 'fortress'; *luel*, possibly a local chieftain's name or derived from the Pagan god *Lugh*)
- Penrith (Brythonic *pen*, 'chief/main/head', and *rhyd*, 'ford')
- Mungrisdale (mixture of Brythonic Mungo, being the affectionate name for Kentigern, and *dalr,* Old Norse, 'valley')
- Blencathra (the tallest mountain of the northern fells; Brythonic *blaen,* 'summit', and *cateir*, 'chair', or possibly a derivative of the name Arthur). Its other English name, Saddleback, refers to its distinctive shape, especially when approached from the east.

Dumbarton is of particular interest in the Kentigern story, being the Brythonic capital of the kingdom of Strathclyde, the region in which his ministry begins to unfold. Dumbarton had its citadel at *Alt Clut*, derived from the Brythonic *alt* for 'high' or 'cliff' and *clut*, 'river', perhaps associated with the water and cleansing goddess Clota. *Alt Clut* was on the *Ystrad Clud,* (*ystrad*, Brythonic, 'wide river/mouth') which evolved into Strathclyde. The Clwyd (*clut*) is a river in Wales; it is curious that Kentigern's legendary retreat and ministry into Wales takes place in part in that river valley where the monastery of St Asaph was later founded. Again, the common linguistic roots become apparent–*clut-clwyd-clyde*.

Christianity in Britannia before Kentigern

Accounts of the late-Roman and post-Roman period in Britannia (around 400–500 AD) suggest that Christianity was in some respects an under-the-radar movement. Some sought to revive the faith among those who had fallen from it at a time of resurgent Paganism, to find new converts in dangerous times and to come to terms with different versions of Christianity in a multilingual, multicultural world. Missionary work seems to have sought to influence whole societies by gradual persuasion rather than trying to scare people through threats of hellfire and damnation. Indeed the spread of Christianity and its central compassionate message appears to have found common ground with the existing Pagan traditions.

There was no organised attempt to convert Britannia to Christianity in the first or second centuries AD. It arrived as a new religion (shortly to be persecuted) with some of the soldiers, civil servants and traders who came to work at this far edge of the Roman Empire. Unlike other cults that were inclined to permit worship of multiple deities, Christianity demanded allegiance to one God only – an issue that put it at odds with Roman imperial authority. That, plus the contemporary decay in Roman power by the third century, meant that its followers provided scapegoats on which to project blame for Rome's troubles and to deflect attention from the real causes. After a century of persecution of Christians, there appears to have been no significant expansion of Christianity in Britannia, except as an underground cult, until Emperor Constantine embraced it in 313 AD.

Despite the balkanisation of Britannia after the withdrawal of Rome, missionary work developed and spread in what must often have been hostile terrain. Yet this is the time – the late 4th century – of Ninian. He was the Christian son of a local aristocrat and had studied under Martin of Tours. He was thus influenced by Martin's development of an early form of monasticism rooted in that of the desert fathers and mothers in the Near East. His mission and reputation in Galloway (through the foundation of the *Candida Casa*, 'white house', at Whithorn) was spread far and wide by many whose names are now lost to us. (There is some evidence that white, lime-washed buildings, signifying sacredness and purity, were used as baptismal chambers in early churches, such as those at Hoddom and Whithorn.)

St Gildas, a contemporary of Kentigern and whose hagiographies suggest he may also have lived close to the Clyde, wrote one of the few surviving accounts of the development of British Christianity. He asserts that Christianity came to Britannia in the reign of Emperor Tiberius – making it a very early date of 37 AD. Known trade routes and early Roman incursions (with troops and traders from right across the Mediterranean) could have made this possible. In 210 AD Tertullian wrote that in Britain 'the Christians have reached regions inaccessible to Rome' and in 240 Origen added, 'The Christian faith is a uniting force among the Britons.' An account of the Synod of Arles in 314 says that three bishops attended from Britannia. By about 350 St Ninian is at work converting the Picts of Galloway. The Romano-British Succath (Patrick) is taken from his home, probably close to the Solway Firth near Carlisle, by Irish raiders during the same period. After escaping and returning home he felt called to go back to Ireland and begin his mission there.

The emergence of British Christianity was therefore well under way at least two centuries before Kentigern. There are records of Romano-British bishops attending religious meetings in Rome and other continental venues. Britannia in the 4th century was the home of Pelagius, one of the most influential and controversial theologians of the era. By the early years of the 5th century, when Honorius essentially told the British that they were on their own, many of the Romanised population of this edge of empire were Christian.

Kentigern was not, therefore, born into a world that was ignorant of Christianity, although he came at a time when there were parts of Britannia untouched by it and others lapsing from it. Here missionary work might have potential among the invading Germanic tribes and there was a possibility of reconverting the many who had abandoned the faith after Roman withdrawal. He did, however, find himself in the midst of a time of conflict and religious tensions and the emergence of distinctly different ways of seeing and expressing Christianity, influenced by local traditions and ancient, well-embedded Pagan roots.

After Kentigern's death (around 603–614 AD) the clash between the indigenous Christianity of the British and that emanating from the now powerful See of Rome (through the mission of Augustine) came to a head at the Synod of Whitby in 664. The one was rooted more in the Brythonic peoples to the north and west of Britannia, while the other was embraced by the Anglo-Saxon peoples mainly in what is now southern, central and north-eastern England. The former had a different liturgical calendar from that of Rome and a different kind of tonsure for its monks and priests. British monks had a tendency toward long hair and beards. The head was shaved, but across the front and top from ear to ear as opposed to the shaved corona of Roman Catholic monks. (The British tonsure was not, coincidently, that different from the style of pre-Christian druids.) British Christians were inclined to elect their bishops by popular demand. Early British saints were called thus not by some complex process of canonisation after evidence of miracles, but simply because they were regarded as particularly holy people. For such saints, holiness was not about being different from others, but about being a catalyst for other people to become different, helping them to transform and live life anew through a relationship with God and Christ. These and many other features meant that, in short, British Christians had developed their own way of doing Christianity.

Furthermore, Rome was not the all-pervasive influence on Christianity that is often assumed. It must be remembered that the centre of imperial power had gradually been giving way to Constantinople as the 'New Rome'. It was in Constantinople at this time, as Bettany Hughes in her magisterial thesis illuminates, that the big debates of Christian theology were being thrashed out (sometimes murderously). Many of the practices of the early British Christians – the reciting of psalms, dress codes, priestly marriage, postures (standing) in prayer – bore the hallmarks of what was to become the Eastern Orthodox pattern of Christianity. Anyone lending an ear to the singing of Gaelic psalm in the outer Hebrides cannot but be struck by the resemblance to worship in the Syriac, Coptic and Orthodox churches over four thousand miles away. Recent archaeological evidence proffers an intriguing connection of trade and culture between Britannia and Byzantium/Constantinople continuing throughout the 5th, 6th and 7th centuries, while the influence of the original Rome continued to ebb.

Thus, behind the surface arguments of style and doctrine at Whitby there was a power struggle. One way of organising church – the British way – was based on local monastic centres, absence of centralised control and diverse expressions (perhaps with a strong Eastern Mediterranean connection and some integration of Pagan traditions). The monastic tradition of simplicity of dress, the possibility of married priests, the inclination to the eremitic life or 'peregrination' (*peregrinatio pro Christo* – 'exile for Christ', to wander often far from home in search of personal spiritual fulfilment and/or missionary work) pervaded this church. Such patterns do not lend themselves to orthodoxy or centralised control. Rome was on a mission to spread Christianity, but it was a unified Roman Christianity built on a close relationship with state power, with little or no space for anything outside that box, especially a western rival.

At Whitby, the Roman way won out. However, after this defeat 'Celtic Christianity' did not die out completely. It hung on, often subtly hidden, up to the Middle Ages, for example in the isolated communities of the 'Culdees' (from the Irish Gaelic *Ceili De*, 'Companions of God'), and beyond in oral traditions, customs, poetry and song (see for example the collection of hymns and incantations in the *Carmina Gadelica*). It has continued to influence ways of expressing church to this day (the Communities of Iona and Lindisfarne for example). Jocelin's 12th-century *Vita* provides evidence that it was still a force to be reckoned with in his time – there would be no need to condemn so fiercely the 'heresies' and 'false practices' of Kentigern's age if they were not somehow present in his own. Propaganda is always an admission that there is something to fight against in the first place.

Celtic Christianity?

The term Celt was first used by the Greeks – *keltoi* – a name at least one of the tribes of the north of Greece appeared to have given themselves. For the first millennium BC multiple Celtic tribes and languages occupied much of northern Europe from the Atlantic to Asia and south into Spain, with many groups, sub groups and differences in culture. Kentigern, embraced as a 'Celtic saint', has become part of the movement to explore and revisit the distinctive forms of Celtic spirituality. Sometimes this has been driven by romantic longing for a 'purer' form of language, culture and faith. Bradley (in *Columba: Pilgrim and Penitent*) writes, 'In our own pick-and-mix culture people are increasingly assembling their own personal spiritual packages in which elements of the Celtic tradition are combined with some New Age nostrums and other bits and pieces.' Bradley goes on to point out that early British/Celtic spirituality was anything but a personal, fluffy, feel-good religion. It was one of rigorous commitment and contribution to community.

It is best to be cautious about a backwards glance, lest it creates a romanticised, idealised or even false version of history to suit a modern agenda. There can be a tendency to try to solve the problems of the present by looking to a fantasised past where everything was in harmony, seeing in the Celts support for anti-authoritarianism or ecological perfectionism. The Celts were not (as many New Age texts and some of the fanciful products of the 18th century and later histories would have us believe) peaceful peoples at one with their environment and dwelling undisturbed in a perfect prelapsarian Eden before the 'nasty' Romans and Christians came along. These were warrior, tribal peoples with customs and practices that nowadays we would regard as violent and oppressive. The story of Kentigern's conception and birth alone, as we shall see, says much about such a culture, its rules and its less than gentle side.

These 'Celts' nevertheless did not seem to have much difficulty in shifting towards Christianity. There is scant evidence of forced or rapid conversion of the peoples of Britannia. As MacCulloch has pointed out, forced conversion was a speciality of the Latin Church in the late Middle Ages. The early church of Britannia seems to have emerged and spread by word of mouth and through encounters with missionaries. Sometimes whole communities would follow the conversion of a leader, while others went along with the faith less from conviction and more from loyalty, or because it provided advantages in trade or advancement among the elite. Thus the emergence of Christianity was, at least in its early stages, much more of a movement than the building of an institution. Perhaps that is one of its attractions in modern times – the perceived freedom from strict theological or organisational strictures. While the church by Kentigern's time was anything but a free-for-all, it seems it had yet to develop even under Roman influence the fully-fledged hierarchical model typical of institutions, a model based on power and control that was to be gradually imposed after the Synod of Whitby.

With the relative isolation and freedom of the developing British church, a picture emerges over many hundreds of years of a gradual integration of old traditions with the new. Grunke writes: 'Most of the saints, who were usually of the upper classes, were once druids. Many sacred Pagan places were retained as Christian sites. Pagan temples became rededicated Celtic churches and churches were built on Pagan places of worship. Pagan worship of ancestors continued with worship of founder priests and saints.' This merging tended to create its own methods and priorities, something that the church in Rome came to frown upon.

Life after death, the Divine as a holy trinity, the concept of a divine son emerging from a heavenly God and an earthly mother … these and other notions were not alien to British Paganism. Bamford reports stories of the great Welsh bard-shaman Taliesin, who asserted that 'Christ the Word from the beginning was our teacher and we never lost his teaching. Christianity is, in Asia, a new thing, but there was never a time when the druids of Britain held not its doctrines.'

Thus according to such accounts we find the intriguing possibility of a Christ figure/Christ consciousness to come already present and providing fertile ground for the eventual planting of the religion of post-Golgotha Christianity in Pagan Britain. Furthermore, in times of conflict and confusion, there may have been a powerful appeal in a new monotheistic belief system that offered life after death and the possibility of a loving God who is 'on our side' instead of multiple gods and fates who must be endlessly appeased. As Owen Chadwick has commented, 'The Roman Empire was falling to pieces and no one could conceive what other kind of world there could be. The circumstances of daily life forced men and women to ask where they could find not only physical safety, but hope in circumstances that looked so menacing.'

Kentigern, as a 'Celtic saint', is thus a modern invention. As we know so little that is certain about him, the blank sheets of his history allow us to project all kinds of assumptions onto him. He would not have called himself a Celt; it is highly unlikely he would even have known the word. Kinship was more important to these early Britons who would most likely have identified themselves as belonging to a particular tribe or lineage. For example, *Owain ap Urien*, someone we will meet again a little later in this story, is named *Owain* (noble, young warrior) *ap* (son of, sometimes written as *map* or *mab*) *Urien* (the name of his father, meaning of high birth, royal). Thus someone like Kentigern, if asked who he was, would most likely have said that he was the 'son of' to indicate his family ties. Alternatively, he might have referred to his wider tribal origins – if Jocelin's account is correct, a child of the *Votadini/Gododdin* who held lands from the modern-day south east of Scotland to northern England. However, there may have been good reason for him to have ignored his ancestry, if Jocelin is right, for he and his mother were cast out and it may be that his immersion in Christianity gave him a new tribe and an identity that was beyond racial or tribal boundaries.

The lack of written evidence for events in the 'Dark Ages' allows us to make all manner of projections not only onto Kentigern himself, but also onto his culture as a whole. The perception of an apparently independent and indigenously generated Christianity, somehow purer and closer to the original, free-spirited, rebellious of foreign influence – all this fitted well with the zeitgeist of growing British nationalism in the 18th century and later. The word 'Celtic', like 'Great Britain', gained popularity especially after the Act of Union between England and Scotland and by extension the already subject lands of Wales and Ireland. A national identity of an imperial Great Britain was being forged that embraced notions of having a special history, national destiny and a unique mission to the world. Thus 'British' emerged as a conflated ideology for the new empire and mother country that swept Celtic Christianity into its grasp.

More recent years have seen the colonisation of all things Celtic by 'New Age' delusions of a perfect spirituality, ethics, culture and social organisation. Some parts of the 'Old Age' Christian church also play into these myths to find meaning and hope while congregations decline. And yet, as Bradley observes (in *Celtic Christianity*), 'the distinctive voice of the early indigenous Christian communities of the British Isles speaks to us through all the layers of distortion and fabrication with which it has been overlaid.'

The great man theory and the invisible woman

Patriarchal cultures tend to see history as a narrative timeline determined by the individual actions of 'great men'. Kings build castles and win wars, bishops build cathedrals, saints establish churches. Such a view is too narrow, for it shuts out the reality that we do not function in isolation and ignores the contribution of the rest of the population, half of course being women. Every story attributed to individuals in the history books carries with it the unheard voices and unwritten stories of those who worked alongside, did the development, set the ground and had the ideas. This is not to diminish the contribution and leadership of people like Kentigern and the individual efforts they must have made, but it is to acknowledge that they did not act alone. Kentigern could not have built 'his' monastery in Glasgow without the countless nameless and faceless monks and lay workers who collaborated with him.

If Kentigern did extraordinary things, the roots seem to have lain in the depth of his faith and his prayer-life rather than in the 'special' powers or destiny attributed to him. Furthermore, the inclination in the Christian story to attribute mass conversion to the impact of charismatic individuals belies the possibility that many, if not most, people come to a faith because of quiet and unsung encounters with neighbours, friends and family or through deep personal insight.

The inclination to subscribe to the 'great man' theory strengthens patriarchal views of the world and leads inevitably to the bypassing of the role of women. The contribution of Kentigern's mother, as will be explored later, often gets ignored. This is par for the course where the role of women was diminished, not to say despised, in a church that over the centuries became increasingly misogynistic. Modern scholarship has illuminated how crucial (not least in New Testament stories) women were to the emergence of the early church and I have documented elsewhere (*Coming Home*) how this impacted on the development of modern spirituality.

The misogyny in Western Christianity reached a nadir in the Middle Ages when sex in any form came to be seen as disgusting or evil and the sexuality of women especially so. Augustinian theology in Western Christendom led to a view of the body and its works as sinful and separate from the Divine. It led people like Pope Innocent III (1160–1216) to state that 'the sexual act is so shameful that it is intrinsically evil' and another Christian theologian cited by Leloup maintained that 'the Holy Ghost is absent from the room shared by a wedded couple'. The 15th-century publication of the *Malleus Maleficarum*, writes Jeanne Achterberg, was the low point of Christendom's hatred of sexuality and of women in particular. Linking the 'sin of Eve' in the Old Testament with the belief that women were inherently evil gave foundation to witch-hunts over a period of 250 years. By some estimates up to nine million Europeans, the vast majority women, were tortured and killed in a prolonged holocaust. Linking sex, heresy and witchcraft was a potent weapon of terror and orthodoxy. By the time the Inquisition left some towns and villages almost the whole of the female population had been wiped out. Jocelin, as a man of his era, seems to have had little time for the contribution of women to his story unless they are submissive and 'virtuous'. Indeed much of Celtic tradition, song and poetry was considered anathema to the later church precisely because it was seen as too 'earthy', too contaminated by its integration of pre-Christian ideas for Augustinian tastes.

The 'great man' perspective may have another downside when applied to the 'miracle-working' Kentigern and saints like him. Reliance on miracles and 'special' people to support faith seems somewhat suspect precisely because it risks making faith and service beyond the reach of 'ordinary' mortals. It downgrades the contribution of quiet lives, simple acts of compassion, everyday gifts of love and generosity, unsophisticated and wholesome belief. We may not have set off and founded a monastery, miraculously healed the sick or converted thousands to the faith, but stayed at home to raise the kids or helped our neighbours when troubled or kept the church building clean ... and many other often invisible ways of service that are no less valuable than the conventionally admired ones.

John Cassian was an early and influential Christian mystic and theologian who died in Gaul. Writing a century before the life of Kentigern he, like many of his contemporaries, expressed a wariness of miracles. A translator of his works (Luibheid) writes of Cassian's view that 'miracles are not to be looked for, they are not to be trusted in … you are never to admire men who put themselves forward as miracle-workers or healers or exorcists. Only admire them for charity. *See if they love.*' Jocelin gives many detailed accounts of Kentigern's miracles and, contradicting Cassian, he sees these as evidence of his godliness and why people should follow him. And yet within Jocelin's often lyrical writing, what Kentigern does and how he behaves as a man shines through. The importance or otherwise of miracles pales into insignificance in the face of Kentigern's character. '*See if they love*'? It can be seen that he does.

Jocelin often emphasises Kentigern's compassion and humility, his abhorrence of being honoured or thought special. Yet, if even half the stories about Kentigern are true, he must have been a resilient human being. He survived in deeply troubled times of war, disease, poverty and ignorance. He travelled great distances, on foot as far as we know, without the aid of good roads, mobile phones, convenience stores or chain restaurants, maps, police protection, hospitals or emergency services. This was a time where the only lights in the darkness were the flames of fires, candles or tallow lamps; a world silent without engines and machines, ignorant of the causes of disease save the attacks of demons and capricious gods, and with no understanding of what lay beyond the clouds except God's heavenly abode.

Kentigern lived and thought in a world utterly different from our own, with only his own resourcefulness, local guidance and the support of kith, kin and fellowship. What thus makes Kentigern an extraordinary man is his ordinariness as a human being impelled by the strength of his faith –

something that makes him 'one of us' and whose example is not beyond the reach of any of us. He knew his way around his world, just as we know our way around ours. Worlds can be transformed by what we do and who we are.

We know little for certain of this man as a thinking, feeling individual, or what his inner life was like, other than what Jocelin reports or surmises, not least in making him so God-filled that he seems to speak or act with little else driving him. One of the risks of the vagueness of our knowledge of Kentigern is that he becomes a receptacle for all our idealised notions and dreams. He had a body like others, with all the things that bodies need and do. He was a living, breathing man – must have had sexual desires, may have been married, got sick, caught cold, had body odours, got angry, had constipation, experienced anger, fear, despair, hope, love … in other words he was completely human. Jocelin's inclination to make him beyond human may inspire some, but alienate others who feel they cannot possibly reach such a standard. Kentigern was an ordinary mortal; in his ordinariness we may find true inspiration.

Jocelin

It is the close of the 12th century and Western Christendom is in trouble. The armies of Islam are closing in on the Holy Land, leading to the recapture of Jerusalem in 1187 AD. The subsequent third and fourth crusades fail to reconquer it. Indeed the last in 1204 was so disastrous it led to the sack of Constantinople, ultimately the schism between the Western and Eastern churches and eventually the fall of the Christian Byzantine Empire. Internal strife continued across Europe and although in Spain the pushback against the Muslim conquests continued, in the east of Europe Islam continued its expansion and was seen as a threat to Christianity.

The Norman conquest of England in 1066 pushed onwards into Wales and Ireland. England was still in recovery from the anarchic wars of succession with Normandy, and three crusades within one century continued to suck up power, resources and attention. The Inquisition against heresy began its work in Europe in 1184 indicating that the established church was alarmed by the internal dissent and fracturing of faith that was under way. D'Aygalliers documents the emergence from the 10th century onwards of many groups right across Europe – the Cathars, Albigensians, Arnoldists, Beguines, the 'Free Spirit' movement and Bogomiles, who were developing doctrines and gaining followers contrary to Roman Catholic teaching. Often rooted in the influence of assorted mystics and wandering teachers, they represented a threat to the autocratic power of the church. The inquisition was fierce in its condemnations and methods, and fires were to be lit under many a 'heretic' and group for centuries to come. Jocelin's writings, an implicit agenda of preaching against heresy, are relatively mild admonitions by comparison.

Between England and Scotland there was relative peace in Jocelin's time, although both countries were establishing their ruling dynasties; raids and wars over a debatable border were common. Churches and monasteries offered a degree of stability in uncertain and impoverished times, but there were rumblings of discontent at their wealth, power and internal corruption. The church needed to reinvigorate the faithful, and it needed money.

Jocelin was commissioned by his namesake, the new Bishop Jocelyn of Glasgow (each is called both Jocelyn and Jocelin in the literature, so to avoid confusion I refer hereafter to Jocelin as the writer and Jocelyn as the bishop). Jocelin seems to have had a reputation for his writing. Certainly his *Vita* is rich and lyrical in its classic rhetorical style – almost like poetry. A monk of the austere Cistercian order from Furness Abbey near what is now Barrow-in-Furness, he had translated or adapted earlier stories for his Anglo-Norman readers including lives of St Patrick, St Helena and St Waltheof. His birth date is not known, but he seems to have been active in the last couple of decades of the 12th and into the first decade of the 13th centuries.

Jocelin was no objective observer. Nowadays we might call him a spin-doctor. He was writing with a specific agenda and did not write biography but hagiography ('holy writing'). The hagiographer gathered evidence from oral and written sources, generally uncritically, added his own perspective, made sure the story fitted the values, doctrines and practices he wanted his readers to follow and the expectations of his commissioner and wrapped all this around the narrative of an individual.

Snyder comments on Jocelin's hagiography thus: 'The sources of Kentigern's life are nowhere near being primary sources … Celtic hagiography in general is seldom ever good written evidence for the history of the fifth and sixth centuries, but it does often give us a good sense of the preoccupations and perspectives of literate Britons from the seventh to the twelfth centuries.' It is with these 'preoccupations' in mind that hagiographies like Jocelin's *Vita* must be read. Although Jocelin had access to an incomplete *Vita* commissioned by Jocelyn's predecessor, Herbert, he glosses over most of it because it diverged from Roman Catholic teaching. Indeed, he tends toward a long sermon on the ignorance of 'those who listen to fables'.

Throughout the *Vita*, Jocelin is quick to point out how everything Kentigern did conformed to the teachings of the (Roman) church. Every aspect of Kentigern's life and the narrative thrust of Jocelin's text becomes a model for the perfect Christian (although, as we shall see, some stories slip through as if Jocelin had not spotted all the implications). Why would he do this?

Firstly, as suggested, Western Christendom was in trouble and there was a perceived need to rally the faithful (and weed out the heretics). Hagiographies in the Middle Ages were regarded almost as holy relics – the reading of them was a means of getting in touch with the saint him/herself. By this time saints were venerated as intercessors between God and people (replacing the ancestors and spirits of Pagan times), as agents of healing and redemption, of support in daily life. Shrines were visited in search of cures, insight, hope of reward in heaven, forgiveness of sins and the avoidance of hell.

Secondly, there is the particular circumstance of Glasgow. Jocelyn had commissioned a massive and expensive repair and extension programme for Glasgow Cathedral in the late 12th century. Money was needed. Strengthening the cult of Kentigern would bring pilgrims to his shrine and pilgrims bring money. The shrine can be found in the crypt of Glasgow Cathedral today, although it is uncertain if Kentigern's remains actually are beneath it. It seems a fortuitous coincidence that Jocelin's *Vita* was written about 1185 after the building work began in 1181. Would some good promotional writing have encouraged funds to flow in the direction of the cathedral's coffers – a public relations technique still in use today?

Thirdly, it can't be coincidence that the See of York that had long claimed authority over the whole of the church in Scotland was gradually eased of its control. Glasgow needed its own hero-saint to substantiate the authenticity of its independence. By 1175 the Pope was persuaded to grant Glasgow the status of 'special daughter' to the papal See, in effect severing it from the over-lordship of York. This contributed to the extension of 'daughtership' to the whole of the Scottish church by 1176. It's not too hard to imagine that one consequence of this divorce-in-all-but-name might have been an attitude from York that said, 'Right, pay your own way then.'

Jocelin portrays Kentigern as a reforming bishop, exactly the kind of hero the church in Scotland needed at the time as it sought to assert its own identity and independence while simultaneously showing that it was following the true Church of Rome. Thus we see in Jocelin's account that Kentigern makes a pilgrimage to Rome, either a historical truth (which most scholars deem unlikely, given his missionary timeline in Britannia and the difficulties of such a lengthy journey in conflict-ridden Europe) or a device to show acceptance of papal authority, an example, which the church in Scotland and the nation must follow.

Fourth, Jocelyn's church relied heavily upon the patronage of royalty; support from the king meant support *for* the king, especially at a time when Scotland was being reorganised to follow the feudal model to match that of England under Norman rule. Both Jocelin and Jocelyn therefore had good reasons to ensure that nothing in the story of Kentigern could sabotage the support of the powerful in royalty or the Roman Catholic Church. In other words, Kentigern becomes a proto-Cistercian, a monk of vigorous asceticism, commitment, adherence to papal authority and hard work to fit the agenda of the Scottish kingdom 'in both political and religious arenas' (Green).

Fifth, Jocelin had other intents in his writing. Nowadays, it is difficult to understand the importance of saints in the medieval period. Kentigern's story is caught up in the trend of the time to provide the faithful with inspiring role models to follow. The saint had to be as Christlike as possible, or at least aspire to be. We find in Kentigern's story many examples of miracles and saintliness.

Jocelin was not writing from scratch. He refers to an earlier *Vita*, possibly commissioned by Bishop Herbert of Glasgow in the 1150s, which covered Kentigern's early years. Only a fragment of this remains in the British Library.

Jocelin's version was written in Latin, an original of which survives in Marsh's Library in Dublin. Unlike the first version, which simply documents Kentigern's birth without commentary, Jocelin prefers bits that fit his purposes and is inclined to add his own moral interpretations, judgements and sermons where the accounts would differ from his ideals or church teaching. Baring-Gould and Fisher note how he 'meddled with his material'. In the *Vita*, Jocelin, on encountering a story with which he is not comfortable, reports but then dismisses it because it is '*Quiddam sanae doctrinae et Catholicae fidei adversum*' ... 'Something contrary to sound doctrine and Catholic teaching.'

Jocelin's account – a summary

Jocelin, according to Henken, follows a common hagiographic pattern used for British saints, which in turn mirrors the Christ story. Thus the saint often has a royal lineage compromised by doubt or scandal, such as extramarital pregnancy, rape or infidelity, that leads to exile, yet hints at divine protection and destiny. Early childhood usually involves being taken under the wing of wise persons or a community other than their own, and there are signs of exceptional gifts and holiness. The saint's life invariably includes one or many miracles, often starting at an early age, especially healing of the sick, bringing people or other creatures back to life or demonstrating awareness and insights beyond the normal bounds of consciousness.

Thus the saint is given exceptionally mature spirituality, awareness and independence. The saint's work also tends to involve pilgrimage, mission, reaching out to communities to convert them to the faith, and advising or confronting kings and other leaders. The stories invariably incorporate battles with evil forces. Having some form of rule over a community or following is also often included, yet authority is not based on worldly power but rather on the wisdom of the saint and the affection and loyalty of his or her followers. Lastly, the death of the saint often involves much suffering, invariably associated with premonitions, passing on an inheritance, ultimate triumph in the face of adversity, being taken by angels and/or becoming 'resurrected' in the sense of being available and still present to the faithful. Kentigern's life tends to follow this pattern, and where it does not Jocelin introduces various literary devices to ensure, ultimately, that the story conforms to contemporary Roman Catholic orthodoxy.

The following is a summary of the main features of Jocelin's hagiography. Jocelin writes, in Latin, as if everything is fact. It is up to the reader to decide on the truth of the account, bearing in mind the nature of hagiography.

Kentigern's life begins with the story of his mother, and later in this book Lesley Orr offers a radical reappraisal of her legacy. Jocelin tells us that Kentigern was the son of Teneu, but says little about her or her part in his life in maturity. Her name is variously and often confusingly spelled elsewhere in literature as Thedaw, Thenog, Theneu, Thenaw, Tenew, Thaney, Taneu, Tannoch, Tennoch, Thanea, Thenew, Denwy, Monnena, Ennach, and Enoch. St Enoch's Square and Trongate in Glasgow carry her name. St Thenew's Chapel, believed to have been erected over her grave, has long since been demolished and was close to the Trongate site. Along with a nearby well dedicated to her it became, for a time, a place of pilgrimage.

Teneu was, according to Jocelin, already Christian, her 'thirsty soul' having come to 'the knowledge of the truth … that was able to preserve her soul from death'. She was thought to have been taught by monks at Ninian's *Candida Casa*. She was also said to be a consecrated virgin, that is, had promised herself as a bride of Christ and would therefore never marry.

She was the daughter or stepdaughter of a local chieftain or king, Loth, also known as Lieu, Lleuddon or Leudonus of the *Votadini/Gododdin*, ruling from his base at Traprain Law. He was a *vir semipaganus*, as Jocelin describes him, a semi-pagan man with dubious allegiance to either Paganism or Christianity. His tribal territory (boundaries were not rigid, there was a mingling with other nearby tribes such as the Damnonii and Picts) seems to have stretched along the lands to the south of the Firth of Forth, west, south and east of what is now Edinburgh. This part of Scotland, known as the Lothians, is said to derive its name from this chieftain. Kentigern is therefore deemed to have royal lineage, but, as we shall see, scandalous parentage.

An earlier tale has Kentigern born of a virgin, a legend that by the time Jocelin was writing was well embedded. Jocelin has immediate difficulty with this account. The possibility of a virgin birth other than that of the unique Jesus was against Roman Catholic doctrine. He gets around this by ignoring Kentigern's paternity and dismisses virgin birth talk as that of ignorant peasants: '... *quia populus stultus et insipiens, in diocese Sancti Kentegerni degens* ...' ('because of the foolish and unwise people living in the diocese of Kentigern'). He goes on to quote from Jeremiah 1:5 ('Before I formed thee in the belly I knew thee: and before thou camest forth out of the womb I sanctified thee, and I ordained thee a prophet unto the nations.') Thus he seeks to move beyond the relevance of Kentigern's birth story and to take his account into the realms of Kentigern's arrival in the world as manifest destiny, chosen by God.

Kentigern's conception is a violent one. Teneu refuses the advances of *Owain ap Urien*, Owen son of Urien (he of the kingdom of Rheged and alleged ally of Arthur), preferring to hold to her Christian sanctity. Turning away from the son of an ally and a politically useful match, she appears to have infuriated her father who promptly banishes her from a life of comfort in his court to live with a local swineherd. Not to be outdone, Owen disguises himself as a woman to bypass the swineherd, who has taken to protecting her. Having gained access to her by subterfuge, Owen ignores Teneu's protestations and rapes her. She becomes pregnant. In his rage her father has her cast from the sheer drop on the south side of Traprain Law in a cart. Miraculously she survives this 300-foot fall. Where the cart crashes at the bottom of the cliff a spring emerges. Jocelin often uses devices like this where *mythos* and *logos* overlap (see *Coming Home*). On the one hand he presents a literal account (*logos*), but opens up other layers of mystical meaning, *mythos* – water being a sign of the movement of the spirit, of God's blessing and presence. Meanwhile, Teneu's refusal to die does not appease her father and she is then taken to what is believed to be Aberlady, some ten miles away on the southern shore of the Firth of Forth.

Cast out to sea in a coracle without a paddle and heavily pregnant, she drifts far from land on the outgoing tide. But then the tide turns; the coracle drifts back up the Firth of Forth and she is eventually beached close to the village of Culross on the north shore of the Firth. Jocelin again reports this as divine intervention. The remnants of a fire, left by some shepherds, warm her and it is here she gives birth. A medieval shrine, in a much-ruined state at the time of writing and now by a busy road, marks the spot where Kentigern is believed to have been born. The date is uncertain, varying between 503 and 528 AD in differing accounts; sometime around the year 520 seems the most likely, although some scholars even put it as late as 560.

The shepherds discover her on their return the next morning and summon St Serf, also known as Servanus, from the local monastery. Meanwhile, back at Traprain Law, the swineherd gets the blame for the pregnancy and is pursued by Loth (presumably an easier target than laying the responsibility and consequent punishment on the son of a powerful ally). The swineherd defends himself and escapes, spearing Loth. Again Jocelin sees this as just punishment for Loth's actions against God's chosen.

It is worth pausing here for a moment to consider the earlier discussion on the inclination to idealise Celtic peoples and culture. Few people at the time got past the age of thirty and child mortality was high. Inter-tribal conflict was common. The class structure was rigid and dominated by (male) royal and warrior castes. Women who secured positions of great power (such as Boudicca) were few and far between. Teneu is the one to be punished for being raped, while the rapist gets away with his crime. The vignette of Teneu's demise and Kentigern's birth (thousands of similar stories are contained in the lore of the time) says much about Celtic life that subverts the notions of a people with noble values at one with the world. As Durkan points out, Teneu is 'Scotland's first recorded rape victim, battered woman and unmarried mother'.

Furthermore, having survived sexual assault, brutal punishment, abandonment, the wildness of the sea, being beached without protection and giving birth without assistance, this astonishing and resilient woman goes on to continue to care for a son and follow him, initially gaining a cultic following and sainthood herself. Yet her story, like that of so many others, is diminished and glossed over, like her paved-over shrine in Glasgow, in favour of the heroic man. Being rendered invisible is perhaps symbolic of the role of women in a paternalistic Church – a legacy that continues to this day.

Meanwhile, back on the beach at Culross, Serf arrives to help Teneu and is immediately charmed by the baby, calling him a 'little darling'. In Brythonic the words are *minghu/munghu*. Thus Mungo becomes the name by which Kentigern is also known, especially in Scotland.

The child grows up under the old man's supervision and is instructed by him in sacred knowledge. Other pupils become jealous of him and kill Serf's pet robin, only for Kentigern to bring it back to life. They extinguish the fire when it is Kentigern's turn to keep watch, only for him to rekindle it using damp, green sticks. Jocelin now shows Kentigern to be a master of life and fire. Another miracle follows in which a deceased cook is brought back to life.

Kentigern's exceptional gifts and his closeness to Serf fuel the hostility and envy of his fellow monks and novices. He resolves to leave the monastery 'having God the guide for his journey and protector in every place' and eventually his wanderings bring him to the hermitage of the venerated but dying St Fergus. Serf, having followed him, pleads for his return. Kentigern is tempted by the love of his old master but believes he must follow divine will and rejects Serf's pleas. The two part 'to not see each other again in this world'.

Fergus' last wish is to be buried in *Glasghu* (see earlier note on the origins of the name Glasgow), which suggests he must have had roots there or known of the presence of a Christian community. Ninian was believed to have consecrated a Christian cemetery at Glasgow. Other versions (Sampson) have Kentigern placing the body on a cart drawn by two wild bulls (a common Brythonic motif), driving them on until they come to a stop and there the burial takes place – in this case Ninian's cemetery at *Glasghu*. Here Kentigern settles by the Molendinar Burn not far from where it runs into the Clyde. Most of this has long since been built over, and the magnificent St Mungo's Cathedral and the great necropolis on the nearby hill now dominate the location.

Jocelin suggests that Kentigern draws people to him and a monastery is established, although it may be that there was already a Christian community on site. His reputation for sanctity spreads and, at the behest of the people, King Morken of Strathclyde asks him to become bishop at the age of 25. He consents and a bishop is summoned from Ireland to consecrate him. Jocelin does not like this and puts the failure to have three bishops to consecrate him, according to Roman Catholic rule, down to the 'foolishness' of the British and Irish and their being '*insulani*' – 'islanders', disconnected or remote from the civilised world, which has led them into 'errant customs'. Jocelin, later in the story, almost certainly invents an account of Kentigern making a pilgrimage to Rome – a device to show his loyalty to the church and to portray him receiving a papal blessing to counter the original 'error' of his first method of ordination.

That Jocelin feels the need to introduce this story and others like it suggests that there were inclinations in the local community to diverge from Roman Catholic teaching – the saint must therefore set an example of right conduct for others in obedience to Rome. However – assuming it is true that around 590 AD Kentigern, when possibly 70 years old, went to Rome to see the newly elected Pope Gregory – Hale raises the intriguing prospect that Kentigern lobbied the Pope to start a 'southern mission'. By chance, not long afterwards, Jocelin asserts that Gregory commissions Augustine, prior of St Andrew's monastery in Rome, to take his 40 monks to what was to become England. After this, Kentigern is said to have returned to Glasgow with the gift of a bell for himself and a crucifix for Columba of Iona.

The gifts suggest another intriguing consideration. The 'great man' approach tends to depict them as working in isolation against great odds. The early Christian communities of Britannia, however, were well connected. There was a continuous exchange of information on each other's work, support in mission, movement of monks from one site to another and the provision of hospitality.

To return to the earlier part of our story: after his appointment as bishop, Kentigern now visits his diocese to find that much of it is only nominally Christian; it is *semi-paganus* like his grandfather Loth. It's difficult to imagine that he would not already be aware of this. At the same time, his relationship with King Morken starts to break down, exacerbated it seems by Kentigern's energetic work and his popularity. Their relationship worsens when Kentigern asks Morken for food for his community at a time of deprivation. Morken says he will only help if God were to help Kentigern move all his wheat from the king's great store to Kentigern's own without touching it. That night the river floods, and washes all the wheat toward Kentigern's monastery, yet miraculously it remains dry. The king is furious at being bested by God and Kentigern and at the loss of the wheat, which Kentigern refuses to return.

In his rage, Morken gives Kentigern a good kicking, but then develops a swelling of his feet and subsequently dies, which Jocelin sees as God's just punishment. However, Morken's successors, 'the vipers of the kin of Morken', do not leave Kentigern in peace for long and renew their persecution. With threats against his life, Kentigern is 'guided by God' to flee south in search of sanctuary with St David (*Dewi Sant*) at his community in Menevia on the shores of southwest Wales.

He moves south first into Galloway to re-evangelise among the southern Picts, who it seems have fallen away from Ninian's missionary work, and crosses the Solway Firth west of Carlisle. There is a disused Kentigern church site (now a private residence) here at Grinsdale on a mound above the river Eden that flows into the Firth. It is interesting to speculate that this ancient site could well have been a safe landing in folk memory for Kentigern. From here he continues along the coastal route south, perhaps avoiding centres such as Carlisle (within Rheged but a close ally or client kingdom of Strathclyde) where he might be unwelcome. He pauses en route to evangelise or more accurately re-evangelise amongst so many who have also fallen from the faith in what is now Cumbria ('He heard that many among the mountains were given to idolatry') and many churches now bear his name (see *The Kentigern Pilgrimage* in part 2).

It is possible he personally visited these communities or it may be that his name was given to these Mungo/Kentigern churches as was customary with the cult of a particular holy man or, more rarely, woman. Nowadays we tend to think of a church as a building, but 'church' really refers to a community of Christian people. In any case, substantial structures were rare in the Brythonic church at the time. Gatherings for worship often took place in people's homes or outdoors in woodland groves or other traditional places of meeting – many with pre-Christian sacred associations. There is some evidence of this in Cumbria. Jocelin specifically mentions one site, which can be identified as Crosthwaite near Keswick with a fair degree of certainty.

He writes of Kentigern preaching to a gathering of five thousand people and erecting a cross. The figure is highly suspect in view of the local population and travel conditions at the time. It is more likely a device to convey a large number and demonstrate Kentigern's popularity as a preacher. There is also the inclination of Jocelin to show Kentigern's story as Christlike by equating it with the Jesus story and the feeding of the five thousand. After this event the clearing becomes *Crossfelde* or Crosthwaite (Anglo-Saxon *thwaite*, a clearing) and the site for the establishment of a later church building.

On reaching Menevia (the modern-day city of St David's in Pembrokeshire) Kentigern resides with *Dewi Sant*. The two holy men form a close bond, according to Jocelin, and their fame continues to grow. Kentigern is invited by Prince Cadwallon to his North Wales territory and sets off with a group of three hundred followers. There, on the banks of the river Elwy (a tributary of the

Clwyd), he establishes the monastery of St Asaph – the latter being one of Kentigern's pupils. St Asaph is known in Welsh as Llanelwy – *Llan* being a common Brythonic prefix to place names, referring to a sacred enclosure, usually round or oval shaped. Once again, in the story of this monastery's foundation, we find that Brythonic mixture of Christianity and the spirits of nature. Kentigern encounters a white wild boar: 'tearing up the soil of the little hill that was there with his long tusk, shaking his head repeatedly and grunting, he clearly showed all that this was the place designed and prepared by God.'

On his death, Cadwallon is succeeded by his son Maelgwyn, who is much less favourably disposed to Kentigern and his colony. According to Jocelin, this had now grown to 965 monks. Jocelin goes into great detail in his account of the monastery, including the division of duties – 300 of the monks, being illiterate, are assigned to work the fields and tend the cattle, another 300 perform household duties to maintain the monastery, and 365 devote themselves to the sacred offices day and night. Maelgwyn's insistence that Kentigern and his community depart is met with divine punishment – blindness. Kentigern has compassion for Maelgwyn, and endeavouring 'to overcome evil with good' … lays 'his healing hand on the blinded man' and restores his sight. Maelgwyn thereafter becomes a devoted servant, financing the cathedral bishopric at the monastery.

While at Llanelwy, Kentigern dreams that *Dewi Sant* has died and has a vision of his reception in heaven. It is at this point that Jocelin introduces Kentigern's pilgrimage to Pope Gregory in Rome. Jocelin justifies the journey by stating that it was so that Kentigern could get the instruction and inspiration he needed for 'the correction of Britannia … to the form of the holy Roman Church'. Jocelin depicts the Britons and their church as infested with Paganism. However, apart from Jocelin's propagandist intentions, his account is very inconsistent. Gregory was not made Pope until 590, while Kentigern returns to Glasgow in 573. Jocelin further tells us that Kentigern made not just one but seven trips in his lifetime, which most scholars dismiss as fantasy and a device by Jocelin to reinforce Kentigern's loyalty to Rome. The number seven is also replete with esoteric symbolism – *mythos* as well as *logos*. It is regularly encountered in scripture as a suggestion of the attainment of spiritual perfection and obedience to divine law. Seven journeys to Rome could be a metaphor for seven inner mystical journeys of deep illumination and expansion of consciousness.

A regime change in Strathclyde, meanwhile, brings the Christian king Rhydderch to the throne. It is now safe for Kentigern to return to Glasgow. In 573 AD, the year of Kentigern's return, there is an account of a great battle between Romano-British forces (mainly Christian) led by Rhydderch and Pagan Britons led by Gwenddoleu. They fight it out at Ardderydd (possibly Arthuret northeast of Carlisle). In this Briton-upon-Briton battle, Rhydderch's army is victorious (aided by Merlin, who is said to have been driven mad by killing his kinsmen in the opposing forces), but it ultimately contributes to the weakening of resistance to later Anglo-Saxon incursions. In the interim, both Rheged and Strathclyde come under Rhydderch's kingship. Although this war is sometimes depicted as a conflict of religions, it was probably much more about a grab for land and power as well as a clash between two very different ways of seeing and governing the world.

According to Jocelin, Kentigern would willingly have remained at Llanelwy. However, Rhydderch, baptised during a sojourn in Ireland, finds Christianity in a parlous state in his own lands. On 'seeing that the Christian religion was almost entirely destroyed in his kingdom' he 'set himself zealously to restore it' and sends messengers to summon Kentigern. The latter, says Jocelin, hearing a 'summons from an angel', feels duty bound to respond to the request of Rhydderch, who offers his entire kingdom to Kentigern's mission. Kentigern puts aside his own personal desires and proclaims, 'My heart is ready, O God! My heart is ready for whatever may please Thee.' Again Jocelin mirrors Kentigern's Christlike nature in his willingness to surrender his will to God's.

Kentigern thus appoints Asaph to succeed him and departs, accompanied by 665 followers. A great gathering of people greets him on the banks of the river Annan at Hoddom in Dumfriesshire. But they are beset by 'phantoms, horrible in appearance' described by Jocelin as Pagan 'agents of the devil and heresy' intent on sabotaging Kentigern's ministry. However he urges faith in God upon them and the evil spirits are banished. At Hoddom a major monastic centre is established, now long ruined, its foundations barely discernible.

A church in Mungo's name is close to the original site, which archaeological excavations have revealed as substantial by 800 AD. By then, Christians of the Northumbrian kingdom had developed, according to Lowe, a cult of Kentigern and Ninian. Like all early British monasteries, it stood amidst a large enclosed site of some 18 hectares – about the same size as that of the Iona monastery. Nowadays a modern graveyard by the river with a few visible ancient stones is all that is left of it. The evidence indicates that the British Christian site was at work well after Kentigern's time into the middle of the 7th century before it was subsumed into Northumbrian Anglo-Saxon culture. With its baptistry and other buildings associated with worship, learning and ordination, it is an indication that places like Hoddom, even in the 'Dark Ages', sustained ecclesiastical authority, functioning systems and missionary work.

Jocelin's accounts of Kentigern's sermons, at Hoddom and other places, show the saint as standing fiercely against heresy. Jocelin writes that much of the country had 'thrown away the faith they had received by falling into apostasy' and were 'stained by the contagion of manifold heresies'. Lapses of faith included clinging to pre-Christian habits. For example, Kentigern roundly condemns the tradition of tattooing or body painting with woad. He argues against another unnamed heresy – probably Pelagianism, a 4th-century doctrine taught by the British monk Pelagius. His theology rejected the idea of original sin and held that people could reach heaven by free will and good deeds rather than divine grace. This created fierce debate in the church at the time, almost causing a schism, and drove Pelagius into exile and excommunication. However, a doctrine of independent action seems to have taken root in the fiercely independent British tribes. As it was contrary to Roman Catholic teaching, Jocelin firmly squashes it and makes Kentigern an heroic proponent of orthodoxy.

There is a further overlap with the Arthurian legend here. After the battle at Arthuret, where Merlin (*Myrddin*) is said to have become deranged with guilt at the killing of so many of his kin on the opposite side, he takes to wandering the hills further north in his madness. About 40 miles from Hoddom is the village of Drumelzier (Brythonic: hill or fort of Merlin). Merlin was said to have had a twin sister, hence his other Brythonic name Llallogan (twin). Jocelin likens Merlin to the legend of the Scottish prophet *Lailoken/Llallogan,* who was also said to wander the same hills out of his mind, uttering prophecies. Merlin/*Lailoken*, so the legends report, was condemned by a voice from heaven to wander the hills and woods of what is now part of Southern Scotland. This region of remote hills, replete with Brythonic place names, seems to have clung to its language into the 11th century. Kentigern was said to have a hermitage in these same hills. His solitude is disturbed one day by the arrival of the madman Merlin who begs for forgiveness for the slaughter at Arthuret and asks Kentigern to baptise him. Merlin dies shortly afterwards. Part of the area is still known as Merlindale. The story may be a symbolic representation of the death of one faith/culture in the face of another or it may be a device of Jocelin's to indicate the supremacy of the Christian faith.

After establishing his See at Hoddom, Kentigern returned to his missionary work in Galloway among the southern Picts, who seem to have had a habit of relapsing into Paganism. Jocelin says that he also despatched missionaries to Iceland, Norway and the Orkneys. Archaeological evidence supports the idea that through *peregrinatio* early British and Irish monks travelled this far with only oxhide boats, *curraghs*, for transport. These wanderers were, after all, a sea and river people, using the motorways of their time. In and before the 'Dark Ages', the waterways were the dominant mode of long-distance transport and the main centres of population were accessible by river or by sea.

After the establishment of the monastery at Hoddom, Kentigern was 'called by God', reports Jocelin, to move his See to Glasgow. The final chapters of Kentigern's story are based here and many more miracles occur. Some of the latter live on to this day, symbolically, in the coat of arms of the city. The robin is a reminder of the time when Kentigern raised a pet bird from the dead, the tree refers to his use of green branches of hazel to start a fire, the bell is said to be that given to him by Pope Gregory. The fish with a ring in its mouth refers to another miracle.

Queen Langoureth, wife of King Rhydderch, is suspected by him of infidelity. He gives her a ring, which she gives to a knight of the court. The king secretly takes the ring from the knight while he sleeps and throws it into the Clyde. Returning home, the king threatens Langoureth with death if she cannot show him the ring. She in turn asks the knight for its return, but of course to no avail. She then confesses to Kentigern and appeals for his help. The saint agrees and sends a monk to fish in the river, instructing him to bring back the first fish caught. Kentigern takes the fish and extracts the ring from its mouth. He returns it to Langoureth, who is then spared the king's punishment. (As an aside, it's interesting to note that yet again it is the woman who faces death and not the man.) There are echoes in stories like this of Kentigern showing Christlike compassion and non-judgementalism, an ability to see and act beyond the ordinary. It also illuminates the crossover between Christian and Pagan morality, Brythonic tribal customs and the relationship between the power of men and women, and divine and earthly powers.

In relating this miracle as evidence of Kentigern's divine powers, Jocelin seems not to have noticed the theological trap into which he has fallen. In protecting and preserving the woman who is the adulteress, Kentigern cuts across doctrines of faithfulness in marriage, just punishments and the evilness of women. Jocelin wants to include the miracle, but cannot square this (and he does not attempt to do so) with Kentigern playing fast and loose with Roman Catholic morality.

Later, in a dramatic scene in the *Vita*, Kentigern is pictured meeting his contemporary, Columba. Whether or not this actually occurred is open to conjecture. Is Jocelin reporting an essentially true story or is it another device to show the possibility of two very different approaches to Christianity (the Irish Gaelic and the Brythonic) working in harmony? Or is it written to suggest that Kentigern is superior to Columba (it is the latter who sets off to see the former) and therefore more worthy of veneration? Columba was an Irish Gaelic man and this would have been his first language, while Kentigern spoke the Brythonic tongue. It's possible they were multilingual or conversed in the shared language of their education, Latin. They may also have had a grasp of Pictish, not least because both are reported to have evangelised among the Picts.

Just before the meeting, the two saints divide their followers into groups of three. As Kentigern exits his monastery, Jocelin records, all six groups approach each other 'singing spiritual songs'. As the story unfolds, Jocelin uses a series of images to hint at Kentigern's spiritual seniority. A follower of Columba asks if Kentigern is with the first group, but Columba says he is with the third group for he sees 'a fiery pillar like a golden crown, set with sparking gems, descending from heaven upon his head, and a light of heavenly brightness encircling him like a veil, and covering him, and again returning to the skies'. Columba then says that it is Kentigern who is 'like Aaron the elect of God', perhaps suggesting subservience to him in the process. The two saints however 'mutually embraced and kissed each other, and having first satiated themselves with divine words, they refreshed themselves with bodily foods'.

Jocelin does not say in detail what Kentigern looked like, although a typical north Briton was fair of skin with brown eyes and hair. He was 'inclined to tallness' and 'of dove-like eyes' and 'beautiful to look upon'. His long journeys, experiences of danger, the privations of monastic life and his longevity suggest a robust constitution. Jocelin has more to say about his demeanour. He exercised 'humility and austerity' in his 'food, his dress, his watchings, in his hard couches and in the mortification of his body'. He would often strip himself naked, plunge into cold water and there 'with eyes and hands lifted up to heaven, he chanted on end the whole Psalter'.

The early British saints had a reputation for asceticism and fierce control of the flesh, such as immersing themselves in ice-cold waters, sleeping on stone beds, and engaging in long periods of fasting or exposure in harsh weather. Jocelin goes on to say that Kentigern held to a vegetarian and alcohol-free diet, although when a guest of others, such as the king, he would 'temper the usual rigour of his abstinence'. His clothes were of goatskin and rough cloth and he wore a stole and a white alb to cover himself, 'so by the whiteness of his dress he expressed the purity of his inner life'.

Jocelin says that Kentigern devoted much of his time to religious observance, solitary prayer and contemplation. At night time especially, Kentigern would have times of 'great intimacy with the Beloved' when 'he poured out his heart as water before the sight of the Lord his God' and purging himself 'of earthly things, he gave himself wholly to the divine above man'. He seems to have been deeply mystically inclined – indeed Jocelin often slips into mystical language in order to characterise Kentigern's faith. (I explore Mysticism in more detail in *Contemplation*). Jocelin writes: 'And so from the golden censer of his own most pure heart, filled with living coals of virtue and kindled with divine love, his prayer passed through the clouds and penetrated heaven as a most clear and fragrant incense.' Time after time, in language like this, Jocelin depicts Kentigern as being in direct communion with God, and says that this mystical communion would manifest itself to ordinary eyes as 'a white dove being seen to rest upon his head' or that 'a bright cloud overshadowed his head' or Kentigern himself appeared as 'a pillar of fire whose brightness when it was gazed upon blinded those looking at it'. Such grace, Jocelin enthuses, was 'like a fragrant cloud' that 'exceeded all fragrances' with 'unimaginable sweetness' that 'imparted complete health to many who were set in that place'.

In another miracle, having no oxen, Kentigern sets two stags to the plough only to have one killed by a wolf. He admonishes the wolf and forces it to take the stag's place. Jocelin is at pains to make this an example of Kentigern's Christlike power to make 'the lion lie down with the lamb'. But this may again be a symbolic approach to a folk memory of an actual event, e.g. Kentigern has persuaded a couple of enemies to cooperate (diplomacy was part of his work as a bishop) and this later became a miracle story.

Jocelin seeks to ensure that Kentigern is always depicted as an example to others of loyalty to Roman Catholicism. However, reading between the lines, a lot of the stories convey Kentigern's inclination towards the many peculiarities of the early British church. Often there is a crossover, with Pagan beliefs and rituals merged with Christian miraculous powers and healing. For example, he erects crosses in many places, but one in Glasgow is so big that 'human genius and help failed' to raise it. Kentigern prays for help and 'that night an angel raised it up'. It becomes an object of wonder and veneration to the local population and has rather ambivalent healing powers attributed to it, such that 'many maniacs and those vexed of unclean spirits are used to be tied of a Sunday night to that cross, and in the morning they are found restored, freed and cleansed, though often they are found dead or at the point of death'. People with magical powers, visitations and help from spirits and angels, the healing powers of stones and sacred sites – none of these would be unfamiliar to pre-Christian Britons. Jocelin's tactic is simply to Christianise them in the case of Kentigern, or to ridicule them as the work of the devil and the gullibility of fools in the case of others.

Kentigern seemed to be a skilled communicator. Jocelin admires how 'in speech he learned to set a watch before his mouth' and spoke 'in weight, number and measure, as the necessary occasion demanded, for his speech was flavoured with salt, suited to every age and sex'. Yet the saint 'preached more by his silence than many doctors and rulers do by loud speaking'. He spent long periods in prayer and fasting. And, Jocelin asserts, occasionally manifested the wounds of Christ on his body.

Jocelin further depicts Kentigern as a stirring orator when the occasion required it, using rhetorical methods, like Jesus, to effect change in people's thinking and break through the bonds of self-deception. Jesus told stories – parables – that sabotaged accepted perceptions of truth. The consequences of this alchemical process are to awaken people to a new, authentic way of seeing themselves and the world. When we wake up to such truth and see anew, it is indeed like we have been asleep or dead – no wonder that the language of all such teachers is peppered with words about being born again, awakening, changing, finding light in darkness and so forth. We can assume that Kentigern used the same tactic himself. In a world where so few could read or write, telling stories from the Bible or speaking from one's own insight was, and remains, a powerful way of getting a message across.

In the Christian tradition this awakening through story has become known as salvation, although over the centuries the meaning of this word has gradually been limited to accepting certain beliefs about Jesus. The result of the storytelling is to awaken us from an ego perspective of thinking about life (which is always deceitful and hypocritical) to seeing the world through the eyes of the soul, a transformation which makes us feel that we are living life anew. Such stories, such parables, are really puzzles designed to trouble and transform us and to convey truth that cannot easily be pinned down by mere words.

Perhaps one of the reasons the Kentigern cult was so strong and his memory lives to this day is that he was a Jesus-like teacher. Anyone who has experienced such a shift in consciousness in the presence of a great teacher does not forget it. Kentigern lived on in memory not because of special buildings or miracles, but simply because he touched people's lives directly, transformed them and set in train an inheritance of thought and ways of being that affected the lives of others down the generations.

As age encroaches upon him, Kentigern develops a loss of muscle power in his jaw. A linen bandage is used to tie it in place so 'that by the fall of his chin nothing indecent should appear in the gaping of the mouth'. He dies in the early years of the 7th century, with various dates specified in the literature – 603, 612, 613 or 614. Other accounts such as the *Annales Cambriae* (a chronicle of important church events in the British Isles composed in the 12th century) say 612, specifically the 13th or 14th January. His saint's day in the Eastern Orthodox Church is 14th January; in Western Christianity it is the 13th. If the dates of his birth are accurate that would place him at death as being around 80 years old, perhaps 100, although Jocelin claims Kentigern reached 185 years.

As death approaches, Kentigern 'fortified himself with the sacred unction and with the life-giving sacraments' and leaves his followers with the commission to 'observance of the holy rule, the maintenance of love and peace, the grace of hospitality, and prayer and holy study'. As he blesses his followers and readies for death he is comforted by an angelic vision. The angel says that as a reward for his life of service and sacrifice he should the next day ask for a warm bath to be prepared in which 'thou shalt fall asleep in the Lord without pain and take thy quiet rest in him'. The angel goes on to say that he should allow his brethren to enter the bath with him so that 'loosed from the bonds of death' they will 'migrate as companions of thy journey and with thee enter into the joy of the Lord'. Kentigern and his disciples follow these instructions the next day and 'along with their holy bishop they entered with him into the mansions of heaven'.

He is given a reverential burial on the banks of the Molendinar Burn. It is believed that his remains lie beneath the shrine in the crypt of what is now St Mungo's Cathedral. As far as is known, no excavations have been carried out to authenticate this. Jocelin claims that even up to his time (the 12th century) 'at his tomb sight is restored to the blind, hearing to the deaf, the power of walking to the lame, strength of limb to the paralytic, a sound mind to the insane, speech to the dumb, cleanness of skin to the lepers'.

The cults of saints were strongly bound up with healing in an age of limited understanding of the causes of sickness. Modern science in the field of mind-body medicine has demonstrated the power of belief and prayer in healing (Dossey). Pilgrims to Kentigern's shrine (who also brought money to the church, one of Jocelin's likely intentions) may have found healing from some conditions simply because of the effect on their emotional state. And, of course, the miracles may not have been solely related to physical changes – healing the blind or deaf or lame may be a metaphor for changes in the way people 'see' or 'hear' truth or learn to walk a new path in life after a period of feeling stuck.

On the other hand, the simplicity of miraculous healing through divine intervention is sufficient explanation for many.

Kentigern: his relevance today

In *Four Quartets*, TS Eliot's profound meditation upon time and spirit, the poet writes that 'we cannot dance to an antique drum'. The mystic–nurse Florence Nightingale commented that 'the law of God is against repetition'. Basing faith and spiritual practice on the examples of the past is questionable. Perhaps it is clear from the preceding introduction to Kentigern that he lived in a world dramatically different from the present. How can anything that he thought or did possibly be relevant today?

And yet, and yet …

As my interest in Kentigern grew and I worked my way through Jocelin's account and the writings of many others on the man, I found the facts, miracles, distortions, projections, falsehoods and fantasies of his life falling away. I began to warm to him, to get to know him, or at least the man I could only imagine him to be. Here was someone whose life and times were utterly different from mine, yet precisely because he was human, ordinary, he lived and breathed and felt like I do. I began, as Cassian urged, to 'see if he loves'. Albeit with different reference points, values, theories of the world and concepts of reality, there he was, a man who struggled like any other to make sense of the world and live fully in it, and to help others do likewise. That's how he loved.

That love was rooted in his faith, the same faith that I was born into and to which I have returned. His story is full of strange and sometimes unbelievable facts if read as *logos*. As *mythos*, it embodies essential spiritual truths that transcend time and place – truths about the human condition, about a life of prayer, about the reality of the Beloved. Kentigern seems to be rooted in his faith *in* Jesus rather than *about* Jesus. His is a story of the impact of what a relationship, a direct encounter, with the divine does to a person rather than arguments about theological dispositions (something that Jocelin sometimes strains to correct). Something in that encounter empowered him to live a long life of service to others and sustained him through all those years as he put body, mind and soul through extraordinary challenges. Something in that encounter made him who he was and touched the lives of others so deeply that his name was carried in honoured folk memory and through place names down the centuries, long before Jocelin put his spin on the story.

If we sieve through Jocelin's hagiography, we find in there certain truths, certain ways of living fully, relating to others with compassion, sharing, and doing faith and church that are as relevant today as they were then. The pattern of life has changed down the centuries, but the fabric of which it is made has not. Kentigern's essential humanity is the same as ours. His ways of being and doing are impelled by the same universal qualities of what it is to be human. His approach to religion, faith and spiritual maturation carry the same essential, universal ingredients still present among seekers of the Way across faith boundaries today. I have explored many of these in detail in *Coming Home* and *Contemplation*. The yearning in all human beings for the 'something other' finds common ground regardless of religious tradition. In Kentigern, the Christ follower, we may discern patterns and commonalities that still speak to us:

1. Soul foods – He feasts on scripture, the psalms, companionship, nature, times of solitude, sacred sites. He seems to know that a life of faith needs constant nourishment, including bodily nourishment. He seems to be careful with his diet and lives a simple life with simple needs, treading lightly upon the earth. Simplicity – of needs, food, dress – helps to make his life less cluttered, free of attachments, so that he can give full attention to and 'feed' on what really matters.

2. Soul friends – *Anam cara* in Irish Gaelic, *beriglour* or *periglour* in Brythonic. Following the Christ path is not an easy journey to make alone; we need the support of one or more wise spiritual directors, counsellors or mentors to whom we can turn for guidance. These guides are people who have walked the path before us and know how to support us in times of need. In Kentigern's early days in the monastery, St Serf acts as his soul friend and later he seems to rely on the guidance of his peers, his fellow monks and rare but deep exchanges with Saints David and Columba. Although her role is obscure to us, his mother too must have been a powerful influence on his life and ministry.
3. Soul communities – He was not alone. He lived with groups of other monks and novices and participated in many other gatherings where he served as teacher but from which he also drew support and guidance.
4. Soul works – He prayed, read scripture, held Sabbath time, engaged in opportunities for learning, and spent time in solitude and silence so that he could hear the call of the Beloved.

These four elements were as essential to Kentigern's following of the Way as they are to us today. They provided him, as they provide us, with the support to discern the true from the false, avoid the traps of the ego and personal will, draw nourishment in faith and go ever deeper in awareness, compassion and service. These foundations enabled Kentigern to:

1. Commit to an engaged spirituality. He did not retreat solely into the life of the hermit to avoid the difficulty of encountering other human beings. He worked with people – individuals and communities – to build a faith-driven life where people helped each other and sought

healing, peace and justice in a challenging world. His was a path of service. He emerges as one of those saints that Underhill describes whose 'experiences are non-temporal, yet whose feet are planted firmly on the earth, the earth of their own day'. He was simultaneously attached to both time and eternity.

2. Undertake pilgrimage. He was rooted in many places in his life, but also followed the call to be a wanderer in service to others and to seek spiritual renewal.

3. Be a prophetic voice. He was a 'truth-speaker' to those in power and encouraged others to seek better ways of being with each other in an often-violent world. His was the way of non-violence; he does not appear to have engaged in military action or carried a weapon, unlike many of his contemporaries.

4. Seek solitude, silence and stillness. In prayer, meditation and contemplation he grounded his faith in long periods of attention to the inner life and his unfolding relationship with God – sometimes with others and sometimes alone. In doing so he seems to have developed a healthy balance of the need for companionship along the Way with times alone.

5. Form church. In participating in the sacraments, singing psalms, teaching and reading scripture with others he brought people together with his faith in Christ as the principal focus. He guided others in the fulfilment of their inner lives and engaged with them to form community and follow Christ's teachings. Church buildings created by these communities came later as people acknowledged the importance of this man and his teaching in their lives. Whether he would have approved of the cultic following that emerged in the hope of intercession for healing is another matter. Looking at his history, it is

likely that later dedication of churches and assignation of miracles or teachings to his name would have been anathema to him. In the emphasis on Kentigern's humility in Jocelin's account, nowhere do we find a request to be followed or remembered. Kentigern was very clear that there is only One who should be followed.

6. Care for others and care for himself. His work was serious, but he seems to have known how to enjoy himself and the company of others. Many of the stories about him suggest a man with a sense of irony and humour. Fun and faith were not mutually exclusive to him. Like all of us, he has times of lightness as well as seriousness. A life lived fully embraces in balance all dimensions of what it is to be human – peace and turbulence, fun and crisis, work and rest.
7. Practise compassion. Often against the conventions of the time, he offered kindness, understanding and non-judgementalism while dwelling in a deeply hierarchical, competitive, patriarchal and even warlike culture. This does not appear to have stopped him from challenging authority when he deemed it necessary. Nor was he a pushover, but was ready to stand his ground in pursuit of truth, justice and compassion, even at the risk of his life. Where some saw competition for power, resources and acclaim, Kentigern saw humility, connectedness and community.

Kentigern, like all holy men and women, points the way. He never claims to be the Way. Commitment to one way permits the possibility of depth in the spiritual life. His life offers us many examples of how to follow that Way. For him the great drama of spirituality was playing itself out between two very different paradigms – the Pagan and the Christian. Jocelin has him firmly engaged with the latter and hostile to the former. But even in Jocelin's hagiography, and being mindful of the culture that birthed Kentigern, we see instead a man who sought to embrace and integrate, to draw people along the Way rather than beat them into it. He may sometimes have used a stick, but he seems inclined to the carrot as well and thus willing to work alongside people in all parts of the very hierarchical society in which he lived. It can't have been easy. Preaching a message of Christian compassion, the humility of a God who is vulnerable and humble, turning the other cheek, protection of the weak, justice for the poor, the equality of all in the eyes of God – well, this must have been a difficult message in the midst of a balkanised province where strength and violence were accepted ways of survival.

To walk the Way in his time must have taken much courage. He embodies heroic qualities, as did Teneu. There is a single-mindedness about both mother and son in their perpetual efforts to survive and to integrate the highest of what it is to be human into the swampy lowlands of so much of everyday life.

I am left wondering what on earth he would make of our times. A world of pick and mix spirituality, global trade, travel and communications, rapid change, relentless technological innovation, ecological degradation, scientific knowledge, and personal and global freedoms, and risks unknown to his times. How would he react to a world so shockingly different from his own?

Perhaps, like Merlin, he might go insane at the prospect of an old world passing and a new one forming that was beyond comprehension. Perhaps, like Jocelin, he would condemn the folly of humanity for falling away from the teachings of the 'one true church'.

However, looking at Kentigern's track record, I suspect his response would more likely be, 'Well, which bit of this mess has a place for me?' And, having prayerfully discerned his path of service for his Christ message in the present, he would likely say, 'Right, how do I do love here?' He would probably do essentially the same things to help people get to God, but in different forms and expressions to fit the times. That's how we do love: the outer form changes, but the essence remains constant. Maybe that's a message for all of us, whatever path we follow. In the time and place that is given to us, how do we do love?

TENEU, THE INVISIBLE WOMAN: HER RELEVANCE TODAY

Lesley Orr

(An edited abstract of an address given on St Kentigern's Day, January 13 2015, St Kentigern's Church, Mungrisdale, Cumbria)

This story takes us on a journey through time and place. It connects East Lothian, where I live, with Fife and Cumbria. But it begins in Glasgow – a city founded by Kentigern in the 6th-century Brythonic kingdom of Strathclyde. Kentigern/Mungo is now that city's patron saint. There's a lovely song called 'Mother Glasgow', written by Dundonian Michael Marra:

In the second city of the Empire
Mother Glasgow watches all her weans
Trying hard to feed her little starlings
Unconsciously she clips their little wings
Mother Glasgow's succour is perpetual
Nestling the Billy and the Tim
I dreamt I took a dander with St Mungo
To try to catch a fish that couldnay swim …
And the tree
And the fish
And the bird
And the bell… Let Glasgow Flourish!

You'll perhaps catch the reference to St Mungo and his miracles, which feature on the Glasgow coat of arms. But who is Mother Glasgow? What woman lurks behinds those words? According to the story that this much loved (and self-loving) city has tended to tell about itself, Glasgow has flourished through its men – saints and shipbuilders, revolutionaries and poets, footballers and funny guys, wee hard men and the occasional Big Yin – and more than a few men of the cloth. The streets and rivers of Glasgow mythology are littered with them: from Mungo to Maxton, Mr Happy to Mr Stein, the historical landscape is populated by a long line of Mr Men. But where are the women? Who is Mother Glasgow, giving perpetual succour to her weans? According to Carol Craig, author of *The Tears that Made the Clyde*, she is all the countless women who have endured at the receiving end of a toxic, strutting, alcohol-soaked masculinity – passive martyrs silently suffering poverty, hardship and violence, but putting on a brave smile and laughing in the face of deprivation and abuse. She is all those hidden, ignored, misrepresented, silenced women who have been written out of the story. But maybe that's not the whole story either …

The image on the cover of Craig's book is of a wee coracle, a big fish and a woman holding onto a boy. Is this Mungo and the original Mother Glasgow – the young woman who gave birth to him in unique and distressing circumstances, sometime in the 6th century? What do we know about her, and what might she disclose about women living in a man's world, about courage and resistance, about faith and passion?

To recover this woman and her meaning we have to go on a pilgrimage of discovery, seeking traces and digging beneath the surface – of Glasgow, and of our own communities. Let's start the journey at St Enoch subway station in a city centre square. It's in front of a glittering cathedral dedicated to consumerism – the St Enoch Centre, funded by the Church of England Commissioners. And if you ask most people about Enoch, they'll answer, 'Who was he?' But the he was a she …

Where the station stands there was once a holy well and a chapel, an important site of pilgrimage and healing before the Reformation. Here's an 18th-century description: 'This ancient well stood near a chapel erected over the tomb of St Tenew, and the ground in its vicinity remained sacred in the eyes of the faithful as the last resting place of the holy woman who had watched the infant steps of the great apostle of the Cambrian Britons, St Mungo.' Despite the best efforts of the Protestant reformers to stop pilgrimages, the well remained a holy site into the 18th century, and the road leading to it was known until 1540 as St Tenew's Gait (now Trongate).

Delving back further, it's clear that the medieval cult of St Tenew was nationally significant – she was included in the Aberdeen Breviary of 1510, which gives an account of her story to accompany her saint's day, July 18. The opening chapter has explored the plethora of names by which she is known, but Jocelin calls her Taneu and the fragment of an earlier (about 1150) *Vita* of Kentigern, upon which Jocelin draws, names her Thaney. In turn, these writings draw on various oral sources and traditions, influenced by Welsh bardic literature, Brythonic myths and legends of King Arthur and his court.

According to linguists and etymologists, maybe the closest we can get to the 6th-century form of name is DEN-weh, or TAH-nayw. And perhaps it's linked to the common Brythonic adjective teneu, meaning thin or slender. The Aberdeen Breviary version, Tenew or Teneu, is maybe how she is most widely known and referred to these days.

So now that we've got the name sorted (not!), what's her story? There are several versions, and as any historian will tell you, these need to be treated with caution. They are not straightforward accounts of what actually happened, and they tell us more about the medieval society and circumstances when the texts were written than about unrecorded events from six hundred years before. But the narrative begins in modern-day East Lothian, as explored in Chapter 1. This was the land of the *Gododdin*, the Men of the North, whose heroic exploits were extolled by Welsh bards Taliesin and Aneirin. According to legend – and the Aberdeen Breviary – King Loth was a pagan warlord, fighting to resist the spread of early Celtic Christianity. He had sons including Gawain, and a daughter Teneu, who had been raised as a Christian by her now-dead mother – sister of High King Arthur. In keeping with patriarchal customs and dynastic alliance-building, Loth decided to marry Teneu to Ewen/Owain mab Urien, son of the King of Rheged, who also featured prominently in later Arthurian mythology. But young Teneu wanted to commit her life to Christ, and to emulate the Virgin Mary. Perhaps she envisaged a life in the kind of monastic establishment headed by powerful women like Hilda of Whitby, or Ebba in Coldingham. Maybe her decision for virginity was less to do with preserving purity, and more an act of resistance against all-encompassing male control over her body and her life, which was the social reality for women of her class and culture, whether Pagan or Christian. Or perhaps that's just me reading back into the story, from my 21st-century feminist perspective – but myths are always open to reshaping for changing times. Isn't that part of their enduring power and pleasure?

Whatever the reason, Teneu said no to her father, and she persisted in saying no. Enraged by her defiance of his will, and blaming her stubbornness on her faith, Loth gave her a choice – either marry and have sex with the noble Ewen (Owain), or he would send her to live with the swineherds, who would certainly have sex with her – a sentence of 'perpetual prostitution' according to the Aberdeen Breviary. She wouldn't budge, and was banished from court.

Luckily the swineherds honoured her faith and personal integrity, but Ewen did not. Like countless men before and since, he assumed his privilege and entitlement to have sex and possess her, and did not respect her NO. He came up with various tactics and methods of persuasion – one recent scholar described him as a calculating stalker – but to no avail. Now we reach the crux of the tale:

> *As she was tarrying in solitude among the swineherds, a certain beardless young man clothed in virgin's apparel violated her in his female dress, and impregnated her in spite of her utmost resistance. And she, constant to her former purpose, dared not divulge to anyone the issue of the affair; but to her father nevertheless it was communicated that she had become pregnant. Then in his zeal for justice he, along with his nobles, adjudged her to be a strumpet and a deceitful transgressor of the paternal law; and they condemned her to be stoned to death.*

According to this version, the man who cross-dressed, tricked and raped her was none other than Ewen/Owain. The 12th-century account has him say, 'It is folly to cry for what is done in sport. Go in peace. It is thy own discretion to weep or be silent.'

For more than 20 years I have been involved in organisations and movements responding to violence against women in church and wider society, and it's poignant – even distressing – to read those words. They could have been said yesterday to girls and women in this country and around the world who are told, when subjected to sexual harassment, abuse or assault, 'Don't take it seriously, it was just a bit of fun. Cry if you like, but just go away and keep quiet.' That's more or less what King David's son Amnon said after tricking and raping his half-sister Tamar. That's what so-called 'Eve teasers' say to women violated in India. That's the experience of thousands who have posted their stories on the Everyday Sexism website.

Likewise, Teneu's treatment by the Gododdin justice system, under the authority of her father. Is the response sympathy, compassion, holding her abuser to account? No – the victimised girl is condemned as a 'strumpet and transgressor'. This too remains the depressing reality for girls and women scrutinised, judged and blamed for the wrongs done to them. Rochdale and Rotherham, date rape, domestic abuse – it's a grim litany. Some time ago I coordinated a research project about violence against women in Christian contexts and interviewed many women who had endured long years of coercive control and intimate terrorism from husbands, including several clergymen. For some, it was the first time they had broken through the shaming silence and isolation of what they had experienced. One told me:

> *For too long I accepted the humiliation and the degradation. I kept thinking about the marriage service: surely if vows had been blessed by God, I should have been helped through this? It hadn't occurred to me that a Christian marriage could be abusive, and that added to the sense of failure and isolation. I was shamed into silence.The devastation of being degraded and abused by the man you love was actually compounded by the fact that for so long no one in church would believe me. So I was labelled as a crazy woman who had a grudge. You've no idea how hard it is when that happens and church and Christianity have been your life. I was made to feel guilty and responsible for leaving my husband, while all the sympathy from other clergy was for him. The church ranks had closed.*

The ranks closed against Teneu too. She was blamed and punished, ordered by her father to be set in a cart at the top of Traprain Law (where people still practise rock climbing) and hurled down the side. Miraculously, she remained unhurt, which enraged Loth all the more, and he commanded that she should be set adrift in a small coracle, without paddle, rudder or sail. This sounds similar to the penalty in early Irish Law for women who committed unintentional crimes – in this case, the 'crime' of becoming pregnant while unmarried – by *preventable inadvertence.* She had been judged to have failed to avoid being raped – maybe she didn't really resist, maybe she was asking for it ... Similar attitudes still lie behind widespread misconceptions about rape and the shamefully low rates of conviction for sexual violence.

But once again Teneu – who according to the breviary 'was not afraid to undergo death for the name of Christ' – survived. I think of her as Teneu the tenacious. 'Upheld by the divine support, she was wafted to the island of May, and thence against the stream, she was conducted in safety to Culross, where from her own bowels she brought forth into the world her son.'

They had arrived 30 miles west and upriver on the north shore of the Forth. Angels and shepherds feature in the story now – the angelic chorus singing Gloria in Excelsis Deo, and the local shepherds bringing Teneu and her baby to safe refuge, baptism, and a life of mission and service with Abbot Serf and his Christian community at Culross. According to legend, Serf looked with compassion at the baby and declared, 'He shall be *Munghu* – my dear friend.' Or maybe he just said, 'Hello, wee darling.' He was christened (in Brythonic) *Cyndyern* – Kentigern.

Somewhere beneath this account lies the widespread popular medieval belief in Mungo's virgin birth, which Jocelin was determined to discredit – his brief was to promote Kentigern as the appropriate patron of a powerful and autonomous diocese of Glasgow, and any hint of heresy would not do. He ridiculed the 'foolish and stupid' locals who believed in the virgin birth stuff.

So the long-neglected and forgotten story of Teneu, the mother of Mungo – and, please note, co-patron of Glasgow – is found in history, legend and devotion. And just as fascinating, for me, is her rediscovery in recent years as a heroine for women in Glasgow, Scotland and beyond – so many of whom have likewise had everyday experiences of constraint and violence; of injustice and exclusion; of homelessness and seeking asylum; of giving birth in distressing and dangerous circumstances. We recognise her victimisation, but in her story there is also space and possibility to affirm agency. After all, Teneu is a woman who courageously acts against the established order of her community and ruptures the surface, laying bare the harm and discrimination on the underside of patriarchal power; she resists and will not accept that the way things are is the way they have to be; she asserts her right to choice and integrity; she faces danger with resilience and faith. I also, in common with others, have appropriated Teneu as a potent symbol of hidden history, solidarity with women, and resistance to the spectrum of gender-based violence and abuse which the UN Secretary General has described as the most pervasive global violation of human rights. She was not the author of her own narrative, but women of faith are increasingly claiming their authority to break through the violence in the silence, to speak for themselves and shape the stories by which they choose to live the gospel promise of abundant life. Years ago when I worked at a local Women's Aid group, I had a long conversation with a woman in the refuge. As she told her story – of marriage to a highly respected professional man who had controlled and abused her for many years – it became clear that the whole family had been deeply involved in their local church. I asked her if she had found understanding and support, and if she had confided in the minister or other members. 'Oh no,' she replied, 'church was the last place I would have wanted to share what was going on. We were all playing happy families. Who would have believed that this pillar of the church was capable of such behaviour?'

I heard similar stories repeated often over the years. One woman had a telling phrase to express the situation as she perceived it. She said, 'There was a tyranny of respectability. Those issues were never raised and church seemed almost the last place for honest sharing of pain and vulnerability.'

That tyranny is finally being confronted by Christian women all around the world. I was privileged to be involved, through the World Council of Churches, in a series of projects and initiatives seeking to address the questions posed by Dr Aruna Gnanadason from India, who has been an inspirational friend and leader in this work. In her groundbreaking book, *No Longer a Secret,* Aruna asks:

'Why is the Church not a forerunner in challenging all the forces that hold women to ransom in a violent and ruthless world? Why has the church been virtually silent on this issue? Why has the church in many instances condoned sexual harassment and even violence in its own institutional life? These are the questions we are asking as we call on the church to respond with resolute action.'

In recent decades, Christian churches (and other faith communities) – in this country and around the world – have started to grapple with the long legacy of gender norms which have given men privilege and authority, while expecting submission and service from women. Sadly, religious attitudes and institutions have too often been conducive contexts for justifying, minimising or colluding with violence against women.

Challenged by survivors and activists to be faithful to the radical message of equality, liberation, justice, compassion and love which they believe is at the heart of faith, many are recognising that churches (with a presence in every parish) have a responsibility and a unique opportunity to contribute to the wider community response – making violence against women everyone's business. There have been reports, policies and guidelines. Local congregations have offered much-appreciated practical support to refuges for women and children or have campaigned against commercial sexual exploitation. Worship and prayers hold these concerns before God; preaching highlights that the promised community is of women and men equally created and valued in God's image. Clergy and other leaders are being encouraged to work in partnership with Women's Aid, Rape Crisis and others – by referral, training and awareness-raising. I'm glad to commend the excellent partnership programme developed by Churches Together in Cumbria to provide training, resources and opportunities for theological reflection to clergy and churches in this area, and with which I'm proud to have been involved.

Teneu has been a source of inspiration for many, not least a network of theologians and activists from five European countries. We received EU funding for a pioneering project to raise awareness, challenge attitudes, encourage empowering theological reflection and worship, and develop resources for action. We decided to name the project for Teneu, after the Celtic woman whose story resonates so profoundly with her sisters through the ages. She found sanctuary for herself and her child in Serf's community. At their best, our own faith communities can offer trustworthy space where victims/survivors feel secure, affirmed and supported in the midst of the pain and chaos. Like Teneu's well, they can be sacred and healing places, where there is freedom to lament and express outrage, to pray and be prayed for, to hear and to speak of God's justice, and to find allies in action to bring that justice to bear in the messiness of human lives. Church at its best offers the context of a community where stories may be spoken with honesty and shared without fear; where there is a welcome for all; where difference is celebrated and pain confronted; where touch is healing, not harmful; where God's grace in love is revealed. We are called to follow the pilgrim way and give honour to the example of Teneu – the Mother of Mungo and Glasgow. In her spirit, may the time come when all people (in Glasgow and everywhere) flourish in sanctuaries of courage and love.

References and other sources of information

Achterberg J 1990 *Woman as healer*. Ryder. London
Alcock L 1971 *Arthur's Britain*. Penguin. Harmondsworth
Atherton M (ed) 2002 *Celts and Christians*. University of Wales Press. Cardiff
Bamford C 2000 *The voice of the eagle*. Lindisfarne. Great Barrington
Baring-Gould S & Fisher J 1908 *The lives of the British saints* (part 3) (facsimile reprint 2008 Llanerch. Lampeter
Bede 1907 *Ecclesiastical history of England*. Bell. London – via Internet Archive
Bradley I 1996 *Columba: pilgrim and penitent*. Wild Goose. Glasgow
Bradley I 1999 *Celtic Christianity: making myths and chasing dreams*. Edinburgh University Press. Edinburgh
Bradley I 2000 *Colonies of heaven*. DLT. London
Bradley I 2003 *The Celtic way*. DLT. London
Breeze D 2006 *The Antonine Wall*. Donald. Edinburgh
Butland C 2013 *Walking into Celtic spirituality*. OSP. Peterborough
Carmichael A 1992 *Carmina Gadelica*. Floris. Edinburgh
Cassian J 1985 (trans. Luibheid C) *Conferences*. Paulist. New Jersey
Chadwick O 1985 in Cassian J *Conferences* (trans. Luibheid C). Paulist. New Jersey
Chadwick N 1976 *The British heroic age*. University of Wales Press. Cardiff
Crichton R 2017 *On the trail of Merlin in a Dark Age*. EFP. Edinburgh
D'Aygalliers A 1925 *Ruysbroeck the admirable*. Dent. London
Dossey L 2011 *Healing words*. HarperOne. San Francisco
Durkan J 2000 *What's in a name? Thaney or Enoch*. Innes Review. 51: 80–00. doi:10.3366/inr.2000.51.1.80
Eliot T S 1944 *Four quartets*. Harcourt Brace Jovanovich. London
Eyre-Todd G 1898 *The book of Glasgow Cathedral*. Morison. Glasgow
Fawcett R 2003 *Glasgow Cathedral*. Historic Scotland. Edinburgh
Finney J 1996 *Recovering the past*. DLT. London
Gambles R 1994 *Lake District place names*. Dalesman. Skipton

Glass J 2007 *The mission of St Mungo*. Athena. London
Gougaud L 1923 *Gaelic pioneers of Christianity*. Gill. Dublin
Gough-Cooper H 2006 *Kentigern and Gonothigernus*.
www.mun.ca/mst/heroicage/issues/6/gough-cooper
Green C 1998 *Saint Kentigern*. MSc Thesis. University of Houston
(https://sourcebooks.fordham.edu/basis/CynthiaWhiddenGreen-SaintKentigern1998.asp)
Green C 1998 *The life of Kentigern* (trans. Of Jocelin's *Vita*, see below) Fordham University – (https://sourcebooks.fordham.edu/Halsall/basis/Jocelyn-LifeofKentigern.asp)
Grunke K 2008 *The effect of Christianity on British Celts*. Journal of undergraduate research 11:1-19.
Gnanadason A. 1993. *No longer a secret*. WCC. Geneva
Hale R 1989 *The Beloved – St. Mungo founder of Glasgow*. UOP. Ottawa
Hale R (undated) *The magnificent Gael*. MOM. Ottawa
Hardinge L 1972 *The Celtic church in Britain*. SPCK. London
Henken E 1991. *The Welsh saints: a study in patterned lives*. Brewer. Cambridge
Hughes B 2017 *Istanbul*. Wiedenfeld & Nicolson. London
Hunter G 2000 *The Celtic way of evangelism*. Abingdon. Nashville
Jamieson J 1890 *Ancient Culdees*. Morison. Glasgow
Jocelin circa 1185 *Kentigern de vita sua* (Kentigern: his life). Marsh's Library. Dublin
Jocelin circa 1185 (copy) *Kentigern de vita sua* (Kentigern: his life). St Mungo's Cathedral library. Glasgow
Jones K 2002 *Who are the Celtic saints?* Canterbury. Norwich
Keelivine 1869 *The legend of St Mungo*. Blackie. Glasgow
Lambert M 2010 *Christians and Pagans*. YUP. London
Laycock S 2009 *Britannia – the failed state*. History Press. Stroud
Leatham D 1948 *They built on rock*. Celtic Art Society. Glasgow
Leatham D 1951 *Celtic sunrise*. Hodder & Stoughton. London
Leloup J (trans Rowe J) 2006 *The gospel of Philip*. Inner traditions. Rochester
Lightfoot J 1907 *Leaders in the northern church*. MacMillan. London

Lowe C 1999 *Angels, fools and tyrants*. Canongate. Edinburgh
Lynch M 1992 *Scotland – a new history*. Pimlico. London
MacCulloch D 2010 *A history of Christianity*. Penguin. London
Macdonald I 1993 *Saint Mungo*. (partial trans. of Jocelin's *Vita*, see above) Floris. Edinburgh
MacQueen J 1990 *St Ninian*. Polygon. Edinburgh
Mackay G 2009 *Scottish place names*. Waverley. New Lanark
Macquarrie A 1997 *The saints of Scotland*. Donald. Edinburgh
McHardy S 2010 *A new history of the Picts*. Luath. Edinburgh
Mersey D 2004 *Arthur, king of the Britons*. Summersdale. Chichester
Mills A 1998 *Oxford dictionary of English place names*. Oxford Paperbacks. Oxford
Moffat A 2012 *The sea kingdoms*. Birlinn. Edinburgh
Newell P 1997 *Listening to the heartbeat of God*. SPCK. London
Nightingale F 1889 reprinted 2017 *Cassandra: suggestions for thought*. Routledge. London
Olsen T 2003 *Christianity and the Celts*. Lion. Oxford
Pennick N 1996 *Celtic sacred landscapes*. Thames & Hudson. London
Pinkerton J 1889 *Lives of the Scottish saints*. Metcalfe. Paisley
Pritchard W 1997 *St Asaph Cathedral*. Smith. Much Wenlock
Rees E 2003 *The essential guide to Celtic sites and their saints*. Burns & Oates. London
Rosen W 2007 *Justinian's flea: plague, empire, and the birth of Europe*. Viking. New York
Sampson F 2007 *Visions and voyages*. Lion. Oxford
Smyth A 1984 *Warlords and holy men: Scotland AD 80-1000*. Arnold. London
Snyder C 1998 *An age of tyrants: Britain and the Britons A.D. 400–600*. PSUP. Pennsylvania
Ross D 2004 *The Celts of the British Isles*. Geddes & Grosset. New Lanark
Russell J 1968 *That earlier plague*. Demography 5: 174–184
Scotland Churches Scheme 2007 *Sacred Highlands*. SCS. Glasgow
Sharp M *Holy places of Celtic Britain*. Blandford. London
Snyder C 2003 *The Britons*. Blackwell. Oxford
Underhill E 1922 *The life of the spirit and the life of today*. Leopold. London

Wacher J 1974 *The towns of Roman Britain*. UCP. Berkeley
Wood M 2005 *In search of myths and heroes*. BBC books. London
Wood M 2010 *In search of Arthur*. BBC documentary.
www.bbc.co.uk/history/ancient/anglo_saxons/arthur
Wright S 2017 *Coming home*. SSF. Cumbria
Wright S 2017 *Contemplation*. SSF. Cumbria

Part 2:

Kentigern – a pilgrimage

ON PILGRIMAGE

There are mountains to climb, deserts in which to lose oneself, oceans to sail ... Sometimes along the way Home we may feel called to undertake arduous challenges in order to 'get' rewards and mature. I've certainly found this in my own life. Yet these mountains, deserts and oceans may also be projections of the inner needs in the search, for within each of us there are indeed the heights, deserts and depths of the self, of the conscious and unconscious realms to explore. Pilgrimage offers this possibility, so that often a great challenge is accompanied by a shift in our perception of self, of our relationship with the Beloved and the world.[1]

My first (forced) encounter with pilgrimage was at school – made to read Chaucer's *Canterbury Tales*. The elements of the classic pilgrimage (the word 'pilgrim' is derived from the Latin *peregrinus* – meaning wanderer, someone from a different place, a foreigner) are found therein: groups or individuals journeying to a religious shrine in search of healing or spiritual guidance. The film *The Way* exemplifies the contemporary combination of a tough physical journey, prayer and worship, encounters with persons and places – all of which inwardly challenge, shaking and shifting perceptions of self, others, faith and the Divine.

Pilgrimage of all sorts, long or short, has become hugely popular again. Well-known, traditional routes like that to Santiago de Compostela (requiring the resources and ability to walk many hundreds of miles) contrast with the trend toward self-created routes, which are almost invariably 'walked' or wheelchaired – the physical, earthbound effort seems to aid the shift of consciousness. I have recently met people going from Durham Cathedral to the Angel of the North to lay a wreath, another group walking the stone circles of the Isle of Lewis, yet another following ley lines to Glastonbury Tor.

It is not so much the nature of the journey that matters, but the consciousness with which we do it. If we travel to any sacred site just to photograph and gather facts we will have a very different experience than if we take a reverent approach seeking to deepen our relationship in God. As the former we are mere tourists, as the latter, true pilgrims. The tourist is involved; the pilgrim is committed.

I once pilgrimaged from Iona to Glasgow. Over 13 days and 155 miles I passed through bucolic idyll and industrial wasteland, stayed in nurturing B&Bs, and some awful ones, traversed mountain and valley, sailed across sea and loch and tramped through bog and along city streets. I met folk of all sorts along the way, had conversations rich or shallow, and was often asked, 'Why Iona *to* Glasgow? Surely it should be the other way round?' Such judgements create dualism: the Divine in this place but not in that place. While creating this pilgrimage, I found myself again questioning the notion of some places as sacred, others as not. Certainly it can seem easier to see the Beloved in beautiful landscapes or loving encounters. But can we also find the Divine in the people we meet along the way who challenge us, in places that are not glorious, or in the detritus in the street?

As I have grown older I have come to appreciate that the sacred is everywhere. There is nowhere that the Beloved is not. Perhaps that is one of the 'products' of pilgrimage – an evolution of consciousness, a realisation that it's not about where we are in place and time, but our awareness of the Divine in the here and now. Thus, we do not necessarily have to endure some arduous journey over great distances and at great cost (in many senses) – even the thought of that can be off-putting. Nor is pilgrimage just for the 'holy'. We do not have to suffer on pilgrimage – to travel halfway on our knees or stretch our bodies beyond limits. The thought that we only gain something if it hurts is suspect.

A short walk to church, the effort to find time and place at home to meditate: walking the labyrinth of our interior realm as well as a labyrinthine journey in physical reality: this everyday interplay of one with the other creates transformation in our relationship with self, the world and the Beloved – this is the essence of pilgrimage.

So it's not so much *where* we pilgrimage, but *that* we pilgrimage. The consciousness with which we approach pilgrimage – the desire to make the effort, the intention, the surrender of the will – is of greatest importance. Through prayer and effort in faith, working through scripture, opening to the guidance of Spirit, all these and more, we come to know that the sacred we seek is within. The outer journey, however long or short, paradoxically takes us deeper inwards. The place to which we pilgrimage and encounter God most readily is in that 'inner chamber' to which Jesus pointed (Matt. 6:6).

We tend to think of church as a specific building and gathering of people going through certain rituals together, believing certain things. Yet there are many ways of expressing church, of engaging with others and the Beloved to deepen our relationships and nourish our path of service. Building church and building the Kingdom are not necessarily the same thing. Today people in all walks of life are drawing on their faith to be social, political and environmental activists – offering homes and assistance to the homeless and asylum seekers, helping out a neighbour or being good role models for kids, volunteering at the local hospital or running a foodbank … in myriad ways people are expressing love and compassion in ordinary, everyday acts. Cassian (see Part 1) reminds us that what marks a person or organisation of faith is not theological know-how or adherence to doctrines but 'how they love'. The encounters we have with others, God and ourselves are ways of doing church that are as alive today as ever. They permit many to participate in the spiritual path who might otherwise feel alienated from religious practices and orthodoxies, or who just need a break from them, in the longing for depth and oneness in relationship to the Divine.

To go deeper into that relationship can be likened to the experience of the mystic. The pilgrim seeks to let go of everyday distractions and interior attachments (*purgation*), to be open to new insights into self and the Beloved (*illumination*) and, allowing all this to integrate, draws ever closer in *union*.

Pilgrimage stretches us at every level: physical, psychological, emotional, spiritual. That's what pilgrimage does to us – yes, does *to* us. Although we do all the walking and organising, it may become clear that it is not so much that we take a pilgrimage, but that pilgrimage takes us. On my own journeys I realised I had not so much sought the Beloved, but that the Beloved had sought me.

A KENTIGERN CIRCLE: NOTES FOR THE JOURNEY

Whether this pilgrimage is made on foot or by some form of transport, I recommend the following:

1. Use ordinance survey maps (the map in this book is not to scale and is provided for basic guidance).
2. Let someone know your route, and provide your contact details.
3. Be aware that many parts of Cumbria have very weak or non-existent mobile phone signals.
4. Take supplies of food and water with you. Many routes are off the beaten track away from shops and cafés. And be warned that not all churches provide toilets!
5. Wear suitable clothing and footwear to match the weather and conditions underfoot.
6. Some stretches of the pilgrimage cannot avoid main roads, so be aware of traffic conditions, perhaps timing some stretches at periods of the day and seasons likely to be quieter. Wear high-visibility clothing, especially on busy routes. The usual road safety rules and country codes apply on pilgrimage as at any other time.
7. There are plenty of B&Bs, hostels and hotels to suit all tastes and pockets along the route. I have not made recommendations; that is beyond the scope of this book. However, I do encourage you to take breaks between stages, with overnight stays if appropriate – and you will also be supporting the local economy, as well as opening yourself to possibilities of engaging with communities and having more time to reflect.

8. It is good to journey with companions, but also good to have times of solitude and silence. Be discerning in your choice and times of company.

9. The route of this pilgrimage is intended to be adaptable. You might try to complete it over days, or split it into sections over weeks, months or years. It may be a combination of a journey on foot, wheelchair, bus, car, bike …

10. I have included rough estimates of travelling times but you need to take into account your own individual pace and abilities, and allow plenty of time for stillness, prayer, meditation and reflection. The length of walks between stages is very variable. If you are reasonably robust, it should be possible to do one stage per day and thus complete the pilgrimage in 9 or 10 days. Some may find the pace of each section easy, others will need more time or to split the journey up and find accommodation nearby. There is no requirement to follow my plan – follow what best suits your abilities and resources.

11. Pilgrimage is not a hike with an end in sight, but a 'slow food' of spiritual nourishment. It is not a race or a route march or a tourist checklist; you do not have to suffer; there is no pressure to achieve any goals, unless you create such pressure yourself. Many people have busy lives and busy minds in which there's not much space for them to receive deeply. I encourage you to create the space to 'let God be God'.

12. Whatever route you take or spiritual practices you use along the way, hold in your awareness that pilgrimage is a time of prayer, in the sense that it is dedicated to your relationship in and with the Beloved. By showing up, in the sense of committing to the journey, paying attention, listening deeply and letting go of your many distractions and attachments, such as 'for something to happen', you become receptive

to the Will of the Beloved. Plan your pilgrimage to give you as much time to be with the Beloved as you can.

13. Let the journey mirror where you are in your life, and notice how this labyrinthine walk sometimes seems hard, the conditions inhospitable and the effort wearisome. Then sometimes feels uplifting, energising and joyful. This pilgrimage will take you through a wide variety of landscapes – muddy tracks, steep hills, rivers to be crossed, glorious countryside and dismal industrial sites. Places of beauty and places of decay. Just like much of life really.

14. I have no rational reason for planning the route in an anti-clockwise direction. It just happened intuitively. You are invited to follow the direction most suited to you, with due adjustment for directions and commentary in each of the stages. It is quite possible to do different sections at different times and taking different directions, but keeping in mind that it is more eco-friendly not to drive back and forth. However, there is something to be said for pilgrimaging according to the sequence I have set out, as there are, for example, distinctive opportunities of beginning and ending reflections as the pilgrimage progresses.

15. Keep a journal of your experiences and use this to support your spiritual life and as a source of reflection with your Soul Friend or Soul Community.

16. Consider leaving a donation in each church along the way, in recognition of the gifts given to you and to support the upkeep of these sacred places for the benefit of others.

Every effort has been made to ensure that the details and descriptions given in this book are correct, but neither the author nor the publisher can accept any liability for loss, damage or injury incurred as a result of the use of any part of this book.

ABOUT THIS PILGRIMAGE

This pilgrimage is not a travelogue, a history lesson, a good food or B&B guide, a nature trail or an archaeology trip. There is already a great deal of information about those things on the Internet and in various other books. The churches, even the relatively modern ones, are treasure troves of historical and architectural wonders (and most provide low-cost literature) and their graveyards often havens for wildlife. The scenery on the pilgrimage is stunning – with all along the way the gifts of nature. But remember, the essence here is to be a pilgrim not a tourist. You may find much to interest you in the history or scenery or wildlife but let these be added blessings and gifts of the Spirit rather than attachments and distractions. Pilgrimage is a time when you can open yourself fully to the Beloved; let that be the overall focus of your intention and prayerful travels.

With a couple of exceptions, I have included only Kentigern churches on this pilgrimage. Many other churches and places of interest are on the same route. You are welcome to explore these if you wish and find your own places of prayer, reflection and contemplation.

The pilgrimage focuses on the circle of churches around the Northern Fells of Cumbria. From the discussion on the life of Kentigern in Part 1, it can be seen that many other sites associated with him would be worth visiting and perhaps incorporating into a longer or different pilgrimage route at some stage. For example a route from Traprain Law to Aberlady and thence to Culross and Glasgow is possible, taking in Kentigern's place of conception, birth and death and the life of his mother, Teneu. Hoddam, the site of Kentigern's monastic settlement before his return to Glasgow, is just north of the border near Carlisle. Further south, St Asaph and Menevia/St David's offer additional Kentigern connections.[2]

A few miles east of Carlisle is the village of Irthington, where there is another St Kentigern's Church, still active. Further east still, at Kirkambeck and just north of Hadrian's Wall, St Kentigern's Church has been closed since 2001, but nearby there is a ruined arch of an 11th-century St Kentigern's Church destroyed during border raids between England and Scotland. St Mungo's at Simonburn, Northumberland, is just north of Hadrian's Wall and about 9 miles north of Hexham. All three sites are on elevated positions with what appear to be *llan*[3], signs of much earlier settlement.

It is not known for certain whether Kentigern personally visited the many churches that have adopted his name. If Jocelin's account of Kentigern's missionary activity is true, it certainly seems possible. On the other hand, it may be that such places merely adopted his name as his cult as healer and intercessor spread. On the balance of probabilities, I'm inclined to the view that the foundation of most, if not all, of these churches, at least in Cumbria, was rooted in some direct encounter with the saint himself.

In total, nine churches on this pilgrimage around the Northern Fells, with one exception, bear the saint's name of Kentigern or Mungo. The exception is St Giles' Church in Great Orton. Documents in the church show that it was changed in the late Middle Ages from a Giles to a Kentigern church, and then reverted in the 19th century. My hunch though is that it became a Giles church from an original Kentigern church shortly after the Norman conquest, as there was a strong cult of Giles among the Normans.

Note: Most churches on the pilgrimage are open during the day. It is as well to check ahead on church and diocese websites, though, in case this has changed. Websites also offer details of service times should you wish to attend. Those churches that are locked during the day usually have a notice in the doorway indicating where a key or access can be obtained. One church, St. Kentigern's in Grinsdale, has now been sold and converted to a private residence, although public access to the cemetery and local footpaths remains.

SPIRITUAL RESOURCES

Include in each stage of the pilgrimage:

- *Times of prayer (beginning, during, end). There are some suggestions below (and in* Coming Home *and* Contemplation*). Don't worry about getting your prayers 'right': pray as you can, not as you can't. Ask that you be able to let go of all distractions, be receptive to the Spirit's voice and guidance, and be gifted with an ever-closer unity with the Beloved.*
- *Readings from scripture, quotes from teachers of authenticity and depth, poetry, appropriate music or audiobooks, and other spiritually inspiring works to guide and accompany you along the way.*
- *Times of stillness in each church; light a candle if possible, pray, be still and silent.*
- *Times of silence and solitude between churches, especially if you are travelling with companions.*
- *Notes in your journal of your responses, insights and promises.*
- *Enough time to take advantage of off-route visits should a particular site of interest or fell walk call you.*

At each stage of the pilgrimage I have added suggestions for reflection, prayer or meditation. Use these if they feel right for you, or simply develop your own.

Pilgrimage allows us to step out of the normal rhythm of life for a while and to listen more deeply to that still small voice within, to see things anew, to reflect on what has been, where we are, and where we are going. Allow time at the end of each stage, and at the end of the pilgrimage itself, for integration.

A reaction to the takeaway fast-food trend has been the development of the Slow Food Movement. When it comes to the spiritual life, pilgrimage is Slow Religion. Quick fixes and the superficial are surrendered in favour of depth and patient maturation.

Consider:

- *How has the journey affected you?*
- *What was it like to be confronted with the familiar and the unfamiliar?*
- *How has the pilgrimage changed the way you see yourself and others?*
- *How has the pilgrimage touched your relationship with the Divine?*
- *To what new ways of being and doing in the world are you summoned?*
- *What new insights and ways of living your life need to be embraced, what old ways need to be let go of, what needs to be retained and cherished?*

Along the way, consider the following (and/or use your own prayers, follow the suggestions in *Coming Home* and *Contemplation*):

Before each stage, ask of the Beloved in prayerful reflection:

- *'What is it You want me to receive?'*
- *'What is it You want me to know?'*
- *'What is it You want me to let go of?'*
- *'What is it You want me to do?'*

The dividing line between illumination and delusion can be a very fine one. Take your responses to questions like these into deep reflection, write in your journal and test their veracity with your Soul Friends and Soul Communities.

A prayer for the pilgrim

Beloved God, be with me on my journey.
Help me to accept what You want me to receive and know.
Help me to hand over that which I need to let go of.
Help me to see clearly and embrace what it is You want me to do.
Help me follow in Your service.
Keep me safe along the way
and help me to see You in all that is.
Set me free of judgements that obscure the truth of You.
Draw me ever closer to knowing You and myself.
May I live in faith and walk in hope.
In Jesus' name.
Amen

Notes:

1. Following the pattern of *Coming Home*, I have sought to avoid using gender-driven words about God, preferring my personal preference of 'the Beloved'. As reader-pilgrim, please feel free to use words with which you are most comfortable.

2. In my wilder imaginings I have often thought it possible to create a great Celtic circular pilgrimage. From St David's, crossing the Irish Sea from Fishguard and following a St Brigid trail north. Then to encounter St Patrick on the way to Armagh, and thence following a St Columba line to Argyll and Iona. After that it would be possible to travel on to connect with Kentigern at Glasgow and proceed southwards, returning to St David's via Cumbria and St Asaph. That would be quite a pilgrimage!

3. *Llan* is a common Brythonic prefix to place names, and refers to a sacred enclosure, usually round or oval-shaped.

THE KENTIGERN WAY

Total (walking) distance is approximately 100 miles.

St Kentigern's
Castle Sowerby
River Caldew
Stage 1
Bowscale Fell
St Kentigern's
Mungrisdale

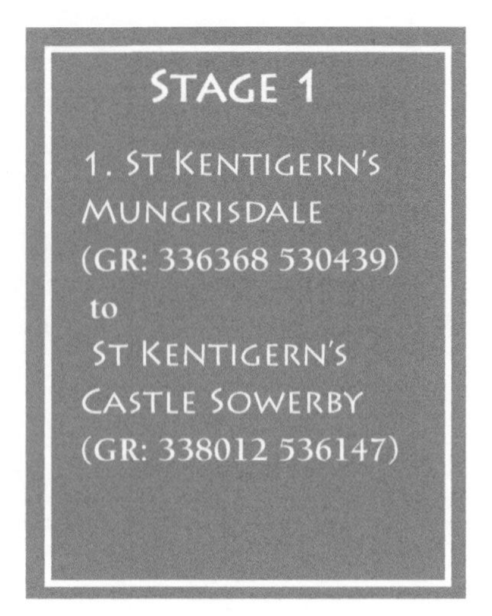

Before you set off, pause in the church and bring the prayerful questions at the bottom of p.99 into your heart and mind. Allow yourself to be receptive to what the Spirit is saying to you.

It had to be a robin. As I set off one wintery morning on January 13th – St Kentigern's Day – there he or she was, perched on the wall by the church. I kept seeing robins en route to the next church. Just coincidence I'm sure, that this bird, so associated with Kentigern's story, was there at the beginning of the journey.[1]

Mungrisdale Church is a quiet delight and usually kept open all day. There is no stained glass or great monuments. I like to think that our ancestors who repaired this church some 300 years ago decided clear glass was enough: the views beyond sufficient inspiration of God.

The walk to Castle Sowerby is about 5 miles and takes some 2 and a half hours at a very slow and gentle pace, allowing time for reflection and taking in the grand views across the Northern Fells. The route is mostly on minor roads, with a short footpath at one point.

From St Kentigern's, Mungrisdale, turn right through the church gateway and follow the road round the bend, and turn right again at the T-junction towards Hutton Roof. Follow this road across the flat valley bottom.

After finding a place to pause safely here, you might reflect upon where you are now in your life: where are the 'flat places' where the pace of your life has felt easy; or where it has felt dull or featureless. What does your faith feel like when it is 'flat' and is this a place where you feel connected/disconnected to the Beloved? How do you receive and/or pass through such experiences?

As you continue along, the road starts to gently rise, past a farm on the left and up to a crossroads.

Rest at the crossroads for a moment. Reflect here upon a time when you were at an inner crossroads in your life. What helped you to determine which direction to take? Are you at an inner crossroads now? What do you need to find the correct turning? What prayer do you want to offer to the Beloved for guidance?

Go straight across, following signs for Hutton Roof/Lamonby. Continue up the hill, a long slow climb, and as you reach the top the Greystoke forest comes into view on your right – and magnificent views of the Fells to the left. At this point your route takes a long arc to the left and over the next crossroads, following the sign for Caldbeck. A view of the Solway Firth opens before you and the Pennines to the east. Stay on this road for about another half a mile, ignoring a sign to the right for Sowerby Hall, even though the church tower of St Kentigern's has now become visible in that direction. About 100 yards further on there is a track on the right signposted St Kentigern's Church. If you are on foot this will take you down a deep cut, often very muddy, to Gillcambon Beck, where you can cross using the ford or footbridge, then to a footpath across a field to the church. If you are travelling by vehicle, continue on the road to the T-junction about a quarter of a mile further on, take a right, and the next right again, following signs for the church.

At the ford or footbridge, pause and consider the preciousness of the access to clean water in your life … In many schools of thought water is associated with our deepest feelings and the depths of the unconscious. Where in the past was making a crossing in your life difficult? What helped you over? Are you being asked now to make some deeper interior crossing? And think of water and its association with the Holy Spirit and baptism. How do you experience the Spirit in your life; how does being baptised, or not, affect your sense of belonging to your faith, to the Beloved?

From the beck the white-painted church stands clear upon a rise before you. Pass through the gate up a short flight of steps and enter the church at your leisure. It is usually kept open during the day. Allow yourself time to savour the interior and exterior of this sacred place, to pray and be receptive to the Presence/Beloved. Bring your hopes and wishes here, open yourself up to the Beloved and allow yourself to be guided and informed. Make notes in your journal for later reflection and sharing.

Note:

1. St Serf had a pet robin that was also dear to Kentigern. It was killed by fellow monks but Kentigern brought it back to life. The robin appears on many a stained-glass window and church banner.

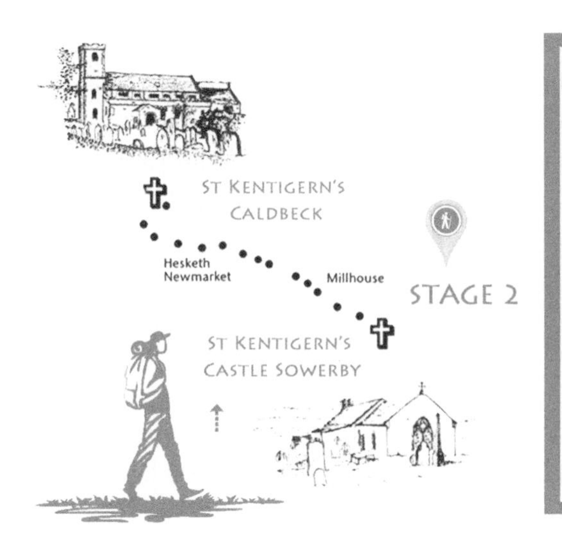

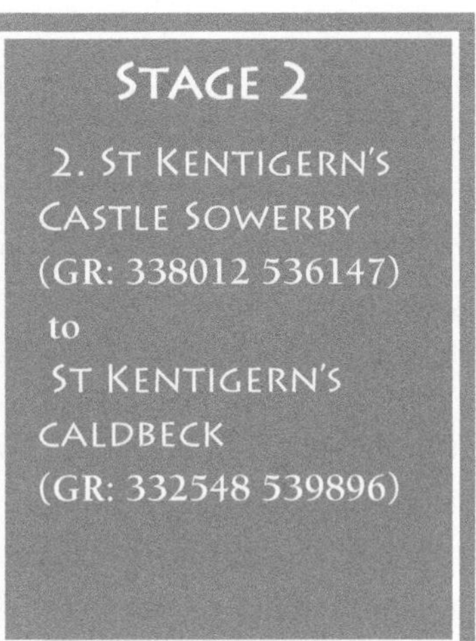

Before you begin the next part of your travels, pause once again and bring the prayerful questions at the bottom of p.99 into your heart and mind. Allow yourself to be receptive to what the Spirit is saying to you.

This part of the walk is about 6 miles and takes some 3 hours at a leisurely pace. The going underfoot is good, being mainly well-trodden paths and tarmac minor roads.

If travelling on foot retrace your steps to the ford/footbridge by which you came and cross back over the beck. At the road, turn right and continue to the T-junction about a quarter of a mile on.

At the T-junction, pause. When were you last at a junction in your life where you had to make a choice of left or right, right or wrong? How did you feel about having to make a stark choice with no grey areas? What was it like if the choice was not clear, where there were many pros and cons? Where did you go for help? What worked and what didn't? Were you able to trust enough in God's guidance, or did you feel on your own? What will it take to help you trust more when you have to make a difficult choice?

Turn left towards Millhouse and Caldbeck and follow the road. Again there are glorious views all around, especially of the shape-shifting Carrock Fell, from one angle seeming conical, from another like a long curved ridge. Pass through Millhouse, over the bridge, and continue towards Caldbeck with the River Caldew on your right. Continue into the delightful village of Hesketh Newmarket with its local shop, post office and pub.

Perhaps a moment for rest and refreshment here. Consider how important hospitality is in your life. Is your home, community or church a place of welcome for the stranger? Do they provide food for the soul? When it comes to your home, do you have open boundaries or is there discernment about who you do or do not let into your life? Let the same question be applied to your church or religious or spiritual community. How far is it welcoming? Who is included or excluded and why?

Pass through Hesketh Newmarket but do not follow the corner round to the right and signs for Caldbeck as this is a slightly busier road. At the junction just after the post office and teashop, go straight ahead for a mile up along the fell side to a small Y-junction, taking the right-hand fork down towards Townhead and Upton. Here walkers will have picked up the marked trail of the Cumbria Way. Pass down a lonning to meet the road into Caldbeck. Alternatively, you can walk or ride staying on the minor road through Upton, then turning right at the junction into Caldbeck. Proceed through the village, with the pub and post office on your left. St Kentigern's Church is on the left set in a large graveyard and is normally open during the day. (John Peel, immortalised in folk songs and foxhunting stories, is buried here.)

Again you will find yourself in a lovely Norman church built on much older foundations and, with a well at the rear, an ancient sacred site. Take your time to savour this place. The well is dedicated to Mungo/Kentigern, though there is some local evidence that it may once have been dedicated to St Bridget, and before that to the Pagan goddess Brigid. The well is to the left of the church, through a gate and by the river.

If you stay by the well for a while, take time to reflect upon the long slow shifts of history that have created this church on this site, and the long chain of peoples who have worshipped here. Recognise that you are now part of the chain. Where do you need the waters of the Spirit in your life? What thirst in you needs to be quenched? Be open to the many stories of water in the Bible, not least the encounter between Jesus and the Samaritan woman at the well of Sychar. Notice this water was freely given, as it has always been. Thus is the nature of the Love that is freely given and has no end.

As you take time to pray, reflect and meditate in this church and its environs, give thanks for safe passage on the journey thus far. Ask questions and journal about your insights, and prepare yourself for the next stage of the pilgrimage.

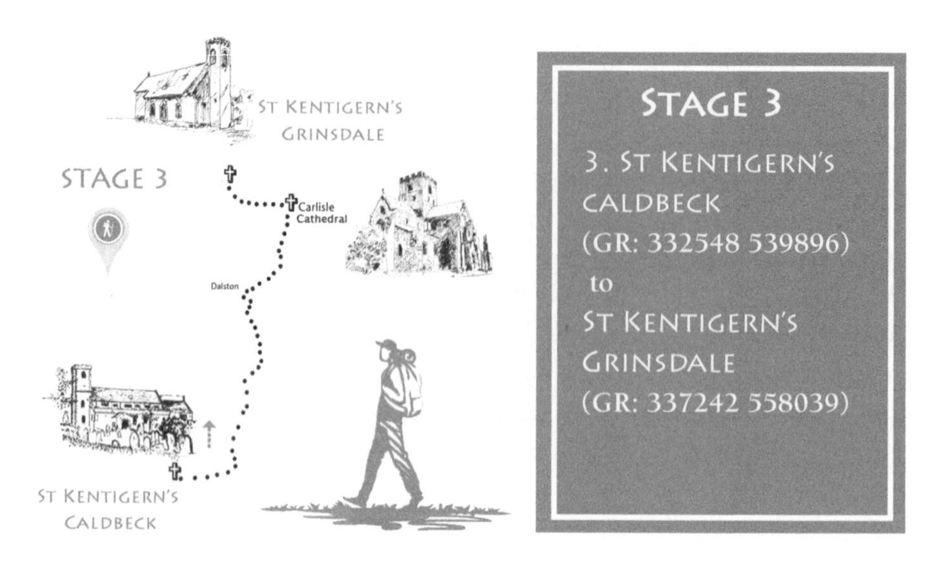

The next part of your journey is a longer one. As you walk or drive from the rural landscape of Caldbeck you will eventually enter a cityscape with all its noise and bustle.

In St Kentigern's Church, Caldbeck, begin your journey as before, with time for questions, prayer and insight.

The drive by road to Grinsdale is some 18 miles. On foot, part of the route being the Cumbria Way – much more pleasant than the many busy main roads – it is nearer 20 miles. That can be too long a hike for some, but there are lots of places to stay and take a break if you wish. A walk, at a steady pace with pauses, to Carlisle takes about 5 or 6 hours, with an added hour for the route to Grinsdale.

Those with transport can drive over the fell from Caldbeck on well-signposted roads to Carlisle via Dalston on the B5299 and into the city, where there is parking close to the cathedral. The route to Grinsdale then follows the B5307 westwards out of the city, past the Cumberland Infirmary and continues for approximately one mile to a Y-junction. Take the right-hand fork signposted Kirkandrews and Burgh-by-Sands and follow this road for half a mile to a sharp right turn to a crossroads and railway bridge. Take the right turn at the crossroads signposted Grinsdale. If you have a car, park (responsibly) in the village. St Kentigern's Church is straight ahead, just outside the village along a track on the right.

For the walker the route takes in part of the Cumbria Way and is well-signposted. Exit the rear gate of the churchyard and turn right, then cross the footbridge over the river. The path takes you out of the village; after some 20 yards take the footpath on the left, which crosses fields and meets the B5299 to Dalston and Carlisle. This is a busy road with few side paths and is not recommended. Instead, a longer meandering route – but much more inspiring – is that of the Cumbria Way as it follows the River Caldew. After 3 miles the path passes through dense woodland with the river on your right.

Consider times in your life when you 'can't see the wood for the trees'. What does it feel like to be lost and unsure of your way or what is going on? When you have such uncertain times, how do you find your way through? What are your sources of strength and trustworthy guidance? Give thanks and appreciation for these. Ask of the Beloved what it will take for you to trust more deeply, if that is needed. Ask that sources of strength and support, the companionship of good friends, the love of Christ and the guardianship of the Spirit be with you for such times.

Occasionally the woodland path opens to fine views of the Fells and the surrounding countryside, then drops steeply down close to the river with its deep pools. Shortly afterwards the way leads through a gate and into open fields. Immediately before you is a big boulder: a seat to take in the views.

Take time to rest on this seat and look around you. The views are lovely. But now close your eyes and look inside you. What is it the Beloved wants you to see in this place, inside or outside yourself, at this point in your life? Is there something you are not seeing that requires your attention? If so, what, and how are you to respond?

Continue the walk along the track to Sebergham Bridge. Cross the road to the left of the bridge and then take the next right onto a mile-long, single-track road, following the river once more to Bell Bridge. Then stay with the riverside path for 3 miles to Rose Bridge. Much damage was done to the riverbanks and bridges during the great floods of 2015. In some places great boulders have been thrust out of place and resist the flow of the river.

What are the 'boulders' that get in the way of your faith and your relationship with the Beloved? What needs to happen so that they are cleared away, or so that your passage around them and the flow of the Spirit is smoothed? What bridges to the Beloved and your faith are important to you? Are some in need of repair? Have some served their purpose and can now be abandoned?

As you approach Rose Bridge there are fine views of Rose Castle, once the seat of the Bishop of Carlisle. This has now been sold to the Rose Castle Foundation and is being developed as an international, interfaith resource for dialogue and reconciliation. In these borderlands, castles and ecclesiastical buildings often merged in function, offering bases for the religious life but also places of protection for local people in times of raids, and bases for retaliation.

What are the boundaries of your faith? How do you feel about and connect with people of other faiths, or those within your own faith with whom you disagree? Is dialogue and relationship possible, or do you need to keep behind your 'castle walls'. Who or what are the 'raiders' of your faith inside and outside yourself and how do you respond to them? When Jesus says, 'Love your enemy', what does that mean to you and how do you fulfil that? Are there enemies you cannot love, and why? Enemies can be inside as well as outside yourself, but what exactly is an enemy? What, if anything, needs to change and what help, if any, do you need?

The path by the river continues, then crosses fields, on past Hawkesdale Hall, for another 2 miles, before meeting the B5299 at Bridge End. Take this road to Dalston (plenty of facilities here for the traveller) but be careful as the road can be quite busy. Pass through Dalston; because of the busy B road, which is a more direct route to Carlisle, I recommend the signposted footpath/cyclepath by the river. This is to the right about 250 yards after the parish church. It follows the river on your right and after a mile meets a railway line on your left.

There is a distinct change in the landscape as you leave behind the Fells and fields of the national park. More houses appear, new industrial units and disused old ones.

Just as in the countryside walk you will have seen broken trees, damaged walls, dead creatures, so as you approach a built-up area you will see more detritus in the street, decrepit buildings or broken machines. It is perhaps easier to see the Beloved in places of beauty, in nature at its most inspiring. But how do you respond when confronted by what you see as dirty, ugly or threatening? If God is 'the maker of all things visible and invisible', how do you hold in faith that which to you might seem anything but in or of the Beloved?

The 5-mile walk into the city brings you to the bridge at Denton. Keep going north, following the signs for the city centre and cathedral. Carlisle is a city that would have been known to Kentigern and possibly visited by him, especially on his route north as he returned to Glasgow, where conditions at the time had become more hospitable to him. The great cathedral stands at the centre of what was a thriving mediaeval community of monks and friars. And the city's foundations go back way beyond Christian and Roman times. Rest in the cathedral to pray and to savour its rich religious history and architecture.

When you think of church today, how do buildings like this cathedral reflect its power, or otherwise? Do you find it more enriching to be here as a tourist, or pilgrim, or both? Is there a contradiction between God in community and God in the church? Do you see churches as serving people, or as irrelevant, or even hostile to the nurturance of faith? Do you participate in a church community? If not, why? If so, how does that help or hinder your faith and connection to others? Do you need the help of the Beloved to find the right Soul Community for yourself or are you content in the one you have?

After spending time at the cathedral, take the path northwest out of the city, crossing the busy bypass using the footbridge, and on past the castle towards the river, crossing a bridge over the River Caldew just before it enters the River Eden. Here you say goodbye to the Caldew, which has been your companion since Millhouse, and start to follow the footpath along the south bank of the Eden. Stay with the river path past the sports ground and on through an industrial area and out once more into fields until you reach the village of Grinsdale about 3 miles from the cathedral. The path ends at the road into the village; turn right here. St Kentigern's Church is straight ahead, just outside the village along a track on the right. It stands on a rise above a bend of the river.

At the time of writing, this church had fallen into disuse and had been sold to a private developer. The building itself is no longer accessible to the public, but the churchyard and riverside path are still open.

The church's elevated position and surrounding walls suggest an ancient sacred site. It is intriguing to consider that Kentigern may have passed this way en route south as he escaped Glasgow. The river is navigable here, and must have been safe enough outside of Carlisle for Kentigern to travel in a boat unnoticed.

Take your time to enjoy this place. If you have walked this part of the pilgrimage, in one stretch you've had quite a journey and may have a few miles to go yet to get to your accommodation (no shortage of these nearby, being so close to the intersection of the Cumbria Coastal Way, Hadrian's Wall and the Cumbria Way). Enjoy the views and the birdlife (and if you are lucky, an otter) by this tidal reach as the river, in her old age, readies herself to pass through the marshes and mudflats ahead and merge with the Solway Firth.

This part of the walk is another ending, and a readying for another beginning. Here in this old churchyard, with its buildings now closed up: what part of your life and faith is dead, gone and no longer needed? Churches, like their buildings, come and go over time. What do you need to leave behind that no longer serves your faith and relationship with the Beloved? What new ways of thinking, being, doing do you need, to build on old foundations? What's your part to be played in the ending of the old and the serving to birth of the new? Pray also for those parts of the Church that are dying: that they may pass away peacefully and that the new forms of church and community emerging will serve in their mission to bring people Home.

Before you leave Grinsdale, you might cast a pebble or twig in the river, as a symbol of that which you want to let go of which no longer serves you and your faith. As you turn to leave, notice, if you haven't already, the fine old beech tree by the gate with its delightful spiral-shaped trunk. Pause for a moment and pray: just as the tree has physically turned upon itself, so we are asked to turn ourselves around in life to fulfil new purposes.

As you take time to pray and meditate, give thanks for safe passage on the journey thus far. Reflect and journal about your insights, and prepare yourself for the next stage of the pilgrimage.

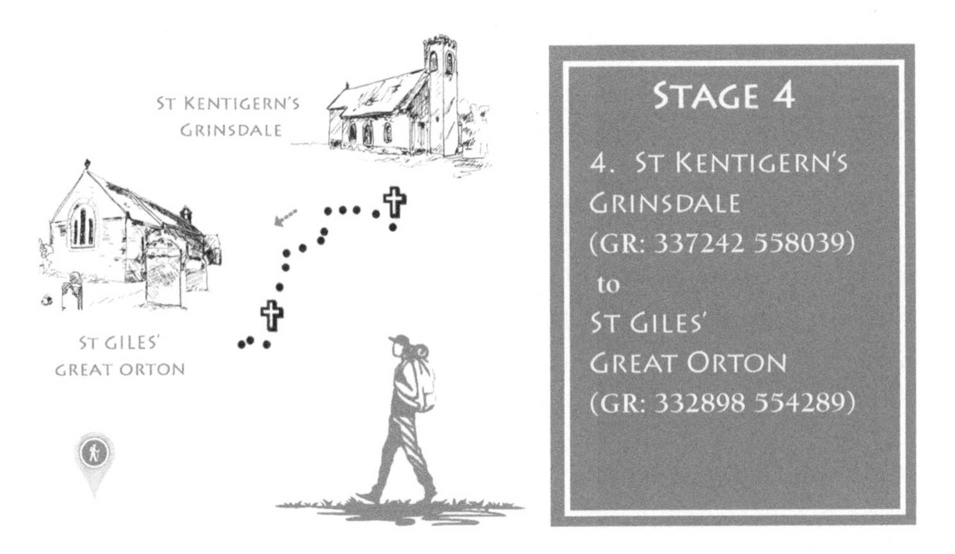

STAGE 4

4. ST KENTIGERN'S GRINSDALE (GR: 337242 558039) to ST GILES' GREAT ORTON (GR: 332898 554289)

After taking some time to prayerfully prepare before setting off, ready yourself now for a very different stretch of landscape from the city and fellscape of the last couple of journeys.

Those with transport can take the minor road from the village to the crossroads at the railway bridge, straight over and onto the B5307. A right turn here takes you to Moorhouse, which is about a mile. At Moorhouse, turn left, following signs for Great Orton for 2 miles.

The walk from Grinsdale to Great Orton is just under 5 miles. Walkers will find it more pleasant to avoid the B5307, by retracing their steps through the village and taking the Hadrian's Wall Path, which leads across fields for about a mile to Kirkandrews-on-Eden. The wall stretched from coast to coast but here has long disappeared underground, unlike the more obvious sections further east. Not a few local houses and farms and maybe some churches will have stones acquired from the wall incorporated into their structures. As explored in the introduction, the wall marked the boundary between the Roman Empire and the lands beyond that were outwith its governance.

We may have inner walls that keep us from each other, from knowing ourselves and as barriers to God. What walls do you have in your life to keep some out and let others in? Are these there for healthy reasons? Does this mean you have closed your heart to some people, and if so what are the consequences for yourself and for your relationship with the Beloved? Have some of these old walls served their purpose? What support is needed to tear them down?

In Kirkandrews-on-Eden, take the left-hand fork of the Y-junction in the village towards Burgh-by-Sands. There, after about 200 yards, take the next left, which is a minor road to the B5307 and Moorhouse, which is about 1.5 miles further on. At Moorhouse, take the first left onto the minor road signposted Great Orton. The church is on your left as you enter the village, and is normally open in the daytime.

It's quite possible that some pilgrims would wish to merge this relatively short stretch with the next, to Bromfield, which is about 13 miles further on. On the other hand, it's not a bad idea to take advantage of a shorter walk to rest and have more time for prayer and reflection.

St Giles' Church in Great Orton is included in this pilgrimage by accident. I'd long had the strange feeling, when I first thought about this route ten years ago, that there were nine Kentigern churches around the Northern Fells of Cumbria. However, my searches at the time within the diocese revealed only eight (notwithstanding the two outliers at Irthington and Kirkambeck). I was bemused, to say the least, when I felt an impulse not to continue to Bromfield as I had planned, and decided to enter St Giles' Church, as it was open for cleaning. There I learned of its curious rededication (see p.97). So here was a Kentigern church after all, the ninth.

Think about the times you have been surprised by God. What has it been like to feel or think something, only for it to come true? What about when you think you have been going the wrong way or have taken a wrong turn and something very enriching happens? And what about the times when you have surprised yourself, perhaps by finding yourself able to accomplish a task, be of service, forgive someone, do something that is against the grain, overcome a great obstacle? What strengthened you in these endeavours? What was it like in those moments when you learned to let go, to trust and let the Beloved take over?

As you take time to pray, reflect and meditate in this church and its environs, give thanks for safe passage on the journey thus far. Ask questions and journal about your insights, and prepare yourself for the next stage of the pilgrimage.

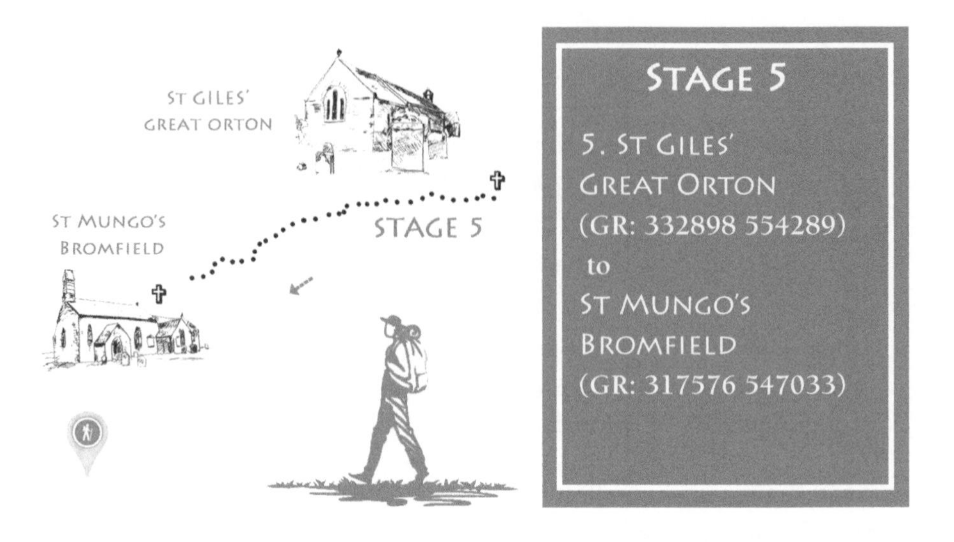

Prayerfully ready yourself to start the next phase of your pilgrimage.

For drivers, there are lots of minor roads on which to wiggle your way across country, or you can simply head south to the A595 and turn right for Wigton, and follow this road past Wigton for about 12 miles, then take the right-hand turn onto the minor road signposted Bromfield.

After leaving St Giles', walkers take the road south from the village and keep to minor roads cross-country to Bromfield. There are very few shortcuts across fields here but you pass along low rolling countryside on tarmac roads, which are fairly quiet. Go past the pub as you leave Great Orton, and after just over a quarter of a mile there is a right-hand turn signposted Wiggonby, with a wind farm on your right. Stay on this road through Wiggonby and onwards, until about a mile past Down Hall there is a minor road on the right to Gamelsby. In the middle of this hamlet, take a left onto the public footpath through the fields to Tarnside, with Martin Tarn on your left.

It's easy to get lost along all these backwater roads, at least I did at one point when distracted by the sight of a fox – and then surrounded by a herd of curious cattle. Have you ever had that lost feeling in your life, lost on your spiritual journey, that is, or the feeling that you have taken a wrong turn? When you look at those times now, with the benefit of hindsight, is it possible that the Beloved was there guiding you, even though you did not know it? Or do you feel God abandoned you then? Do you sometimes feel lost and abandoned now? What helps you find your true direction? What helps you to trust more deeply? Where do you go for sources of support? Mother Julian of Norwich wrote, 'All shall be well, and all manner of thing shall be well.' Can you imagine trusting that deeply? If not, what needs to change in your life so that you can?

After you pass the tarn, take a right at the junction and stay on this long straight road for 3 miles, over a crossroads, then onwards, until the road takes a sharp left into the hamlet of Lessonhall. To avoid a fairly busy B5302, with no safe side paths to walk, take the first right and then the next left in Lessonhall and follow this lane around to Dundraw. Take a right at the first junction in Dundraw, and follow the minor roads and lanes as they arc round to Wheyrigg.

Take your time along these roads and enjoy the views to the east. You can see the massif of the Northern Fells with Carrock Fell in the distance, the tip of Blencathra, then Skiddaw sticking its nose up into the air to the southeast – you are now on the opposite side of the Fells whence you started. As you walk on to Wheyrigg you will meet the B5302 at a T-junction, where you turn right, then immediately left towards Blencogo. The road takes a sharp right into Blencogo; follow this road for 2 miles, through the village, and go straight on to Bromfield. St Mungo's Church is on your right. On my recent visits this church has been locked, so it would be a good idea to check the diocese website (www.carlislediocese.org.uk) beforehand for access.

In Handel's oratorio The Messiah, *a soloist sings the biblical refrain 'Make straight in the desert a highway for our God'. You have just walked or driven quite a roundabout route from Great Orton. What has your journey towards God been like? What do you need to 'make straight the way'? What distractions or obstructions keep you from staying focused on your relationship with the Beloved. Are there times of 'Now I'm shopping' or 'at work', or any other daily activity? Then times of, 'Now I'm with God.' What will it take to help shift your awareness out of this duality, so that you are more in relationship with the Beloved; so that you live more deeply aware of the reality that there is nowhere that God is not?*

In the field at the rear of the church is St Mungo's Well. Springs have been sacred sites for millennia. The church has evidence of wooden and stone foundations going back to Roman times. It therefore predates Kentigern. Perhaps he visited it, and maybe even helped to restore it and rebuild its community if, as Jocelin writes, the people had 'lapsed into Paganism'. The well is now capped and the land around it extremely boggy, at least it was on the occasion I last visited. A dead kestrel added to the foetid water. But life finds a way. A pair of swallows had nested and built their little mud cup under the well cap. The chicks looked at me looking at them. New life was growing even in a seemingly inhospitable place.

Consider the blessing of clean water in your life. Consider too how the water of life, the Holy Spirit, has touched you down the years. Do you feel that touch in your life today? How does it touch you as you walk this pilgrimage? Are there things from which you still need grace to wash you clean? Have you been baptised? If not, are you feeling ready for such a commitment? Take time to pray and reflect on how to be more receptive to the Spirit, so that anything that gets in the way of your relationship with the Beloved can be washed clean or away.

As you take time to pray, reflect and meditate in this church and its environs, give thanks for safe passage on the journey thus far. Ask questions and journal about your insights, and prepare yourself for the next stage of the pilgrimage.

As usual, before you set off, take time for preparation and prayer.

Those with transport can take a short trip along pleasant country lanes through Langrigg, Westnewton, and then on the B5301 to Aspatria. St Kentigern's Church is by the main road in the centre of the town. Walkers can follow much the same route – but it is especially desirable to avoid the very busy A596, which, other than in Aspatria, has few footpaths alongside. The journey on foot is just under 5 miles and takes about 2-3 hours at a steady pace, allowing time to be prayerful, still and reflective.

From Bromfield Church, go to the crossroads in the centre of the village and take a right turn to Langrigg, which is about a mile. This minor road is fairly quiet. At the T-junction in Langrigg, turn right and then, after about 100 yards, take the next left, signposted Westnewton. Along the way there are fine views of the mountains to the east (watch them change shape as your pilgrimage progresses to different vantage points) and the Solway Firth to the west. Now you are between sea and land.

How the sea calls us! Have you noticed how when close to the sea we always look to it? How when we build houses nearby, they are invariably planned to face towards it. Our bodies are about 60% salt water. We carry the sea within us. In the womb, we are immersed in the sea. What does it feel like to be made of something yet separate from it? Is that perhaps what it can feel like in our relationship to the Beloved? And here, not far from the sea, the land is on the edge. What has it been like in your life to feel like you are on the edge? Frightening? Thrilling? Does it feel like that now? When you have gone to the edge in your life in a tough way, what stopped you falling over? What did you learn from that about your relationship with the Divine? How does that experience inform that relationship and your faith now?

At the next T-junction, turn right and follow this minor road for 2 miles, at which point it joins the B5301. Bear left here into the village of Westnewton. Pass through the village, staying with the B5301 for the next mile and a half through Yearngill and directly into Aspatria. As you approach the town you can see the church directly ahead of you. There is a Y-junction before you, bear left towards the church. You can enter the churchyard here by the rear gate at the roadside or pass by to the T-junction at the A596 a few yards further on. The main entrance to St Kentigern's Church is to the right on a rise above the road. Here a relatively modern (1840s) church stands on much earlier Norman foundations and possibly much earlier origins than that. The church is normally open during the day. There is also a holy well in the churchyard.

Nowadays we might go to great lengths to preserve old buildings. So it is curious how many churches were demolished and replaced down the years, especially in the Victorian era. A reflection in this church might take account of how buildings come and go, but that 'the church' is not the building: it is the community of people. In Kentigern's time it was common to be at a church meeting at best in a wooden structure, or gathered in a grove or out in the open air. The 'peregrinators' like Kentigern took church out to where the people were, as well as constructing monasteries and churches. If you are part of a church, is it about an encounter between people for worship and prayer and an encouragement to approach the Beloved? Or do you have to spend a lot of time and resources maintaining buildings at the expense of personal contact? What bits of your old beliefs have become false to fact and need to be allowed to pass away so you can embrace the Beloved more nearly?

Many churches today stand empty or are little used. And yet, at times of crisis when people feel the need to come together, or to mark rites of passage such as weddings and funerals, churches still have relevance for many. In these changing times, new ways of expressing church are being formed. Perhaps these fresh expressions will find ways to integrate the old and the new, maintaining the precious continuity of faith that so many of these old buildings, with all their limitations and rich stories, represent.

As you take time to pray, reflect and meditate in this church and its environs, give thanks for safe passage on the journey thus far. Ask questions and journal about your insights, and prepare yourself for the next stage of the pilgrimage.

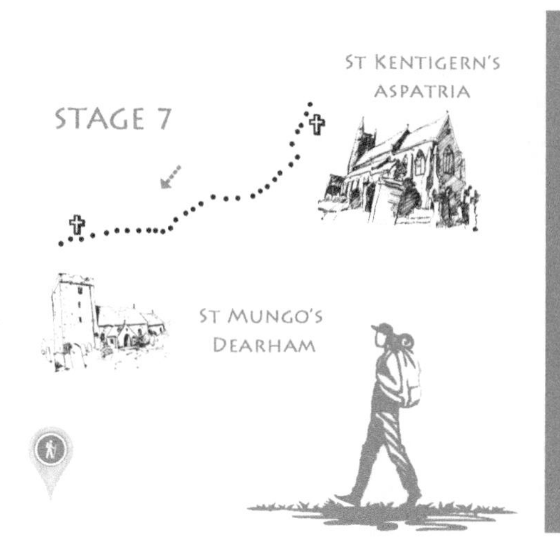

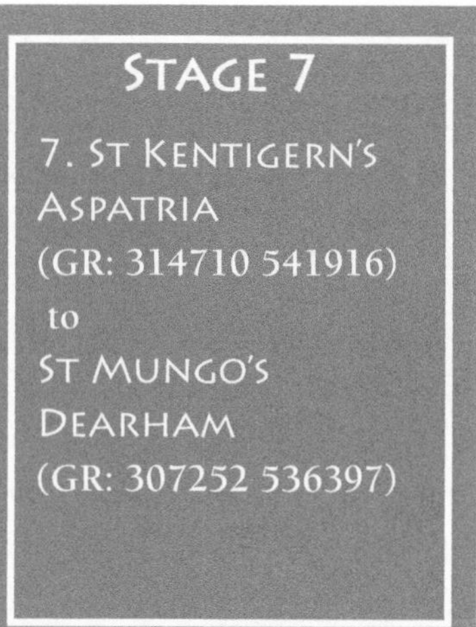

As usual, take some time for prayer and reflection before starting out.

From here to our next church (another St Mungo's) in Dearham, the walk is about 10 miles, taking into account a slightly longer route to avoid the busy A596 (which has long stretches without footpaths). Drivers can take the A596 from Aspatria to Crosby, turning left onto a minor road as they pass out of Crosby, and follow the signposts for Dearham. As you enter Dearham, take the first left turn towards the church.

Pilgrims on foot can cross the A596 in front of St Kentigern's Church and walk along through the town, then take the left turn south signposted Arkleby. About a quarter of a mile walk skirts the railway station and some small-business buildings and passes over a railway bridge. The road is a, usually quiet, continuation of the B5301. There are no significant off-road tracks to Dearham, but most of these country lanes have only light traffic. Once again there are lovely views across the Solway Firth. A mile-long walk crosses the River Ellen and takes you to a T-junction just outside of Arkleby. Turn right here, and right again a few yards further on at the Y-junction towards the village of Gilcrux, which is 2 miles further on.

You might find a spot to rest here. Gilcrux is another place echoing the early peoples of the landscape you are passing through, for the name, meaning 'hill retreat', is derived from the Brythonic. Are there things in your life you need to retreat from, in order to disengage or to find better ways of dealing with them? Do you have time to go on a spiritual retreat from time to time (perhaps this pilgrimage has that quality for you) so that you can get yourself taken care of and have time just to be with the Beloved without distractions?

From Gilcrux, continue along the main road following signs for Cockermouth/Tallentire. Half a mile after Gilcrux, there is a T-junction at Greengill; take the left turn here and then, about 100 yards further on, the next right for Dearham. In Dearham, follow the main street through the village round to the right for a quarter of a mile and the church is signposted on Church Street on the right. St Mungo's Church is (at the time of writing) locked during the day, but there is a sign with a telephone contact for access. Inside, there is a Viking wheel cross, almost five feet tall.

These Vikings had not come to raid and leave, like a century earlier, but to settle. They established communities and raised crosses, not dissimilar to the great crosses, known as 'Celtic' crosses, of Iona, which they had also raided. Something in the Christian message touched them enough to want to abandon their panoply of gods and embrace the One. How ironic that the destroyers became the builders.

Whence cometh your faith? Did you grow into a relationship with the Beloved? Or did you experience a sudden conversion? What is that relationship like now? As faith requires service, reflect upon how you put your beliefs into action. How do you serve? How do you pass your beliefs/faith on to others? Through the way you live your life? Through trying to convert others? How do others react to the way you express your faith?

As you take time to pray, reflect and meditate in this church and its environs, give thanks for safe passage on the journey thus far. Ask questions and journal about your insights, and prepare yourself for the next stage of the pilgrimage.

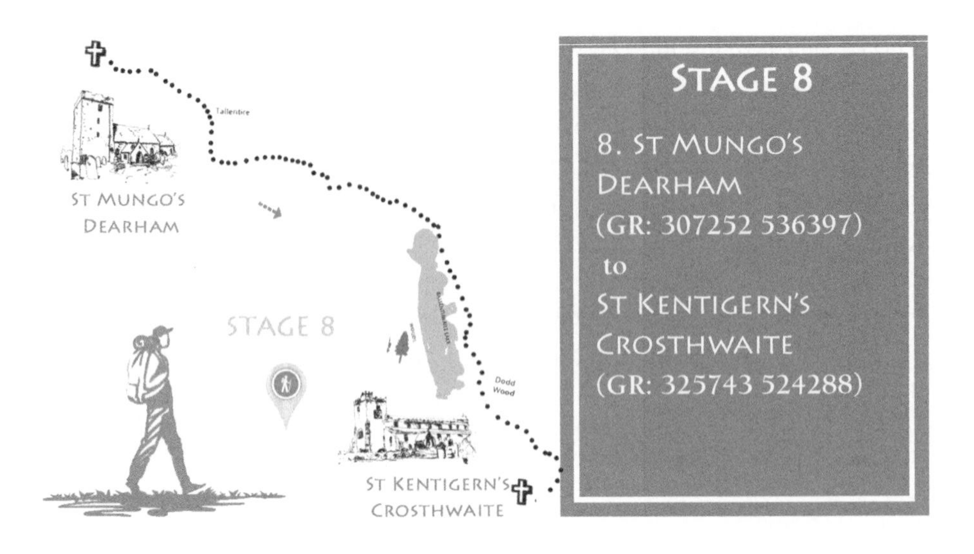

As usual, take some time for prayer and reflection before starting out.

This is by far the longest part of our pilgrimage. By vehicle it is quite straightforward, almost 18 miles from Dearham to Keswick/Crosthwaite (unless you choose to detour to some of the churches and landmarks on the walkers' route). Take the road back through Dearham high street and veer right towards the A594. At the crossroads with this A-road, turn left onto the A595 and continue to the next roundabout. Then turn right here onto the A66 and continue to the next roundabout. Turn left here following signs for Keswick, and continue for 13 miles with Bassenthwaite Lake on your left. Turn off at the junction of the A66 and the B5289 towards Keswick. A third of a mile down the road there is a left turn, and St Kentigern's Church, Crosthwaite is visible on a rise at the head of a cul-de-sac.

On foot the pilgrimage is about 22 miles, with the route often cross-country to avoid busy main roads. Allow at least 8 hours for the journey, according to your abilities, permitting time for 'slow faith' work along the way. Some may take this distance in their stride, but it was definitely at this pilgrim's limits. There is no shortage of places to stay along the way, indeed at any point on this pilgrimage, Cumbria having a strong tourist industry.

Retrace your steps down Dearham high street and round to the right for about a quarter of a mile, and walk towards Gilcrux. In another quarter of a mile there is a footpath on your right towards Low House. Follow the footpath over the fields to Tallentire, a name with Brythonic/Celtic roots meaning 'land/world's end'. Once again you are amidst evidence of an ancient culture and language now lost, but supporting Nora Chadwick's assertion, cited in Part 1, that Kentigern would have been able to make himself understood along the length of western England and into Wales and southern Scotland.

One of the certainties of life is change. Historically massive paradigm shifts occur across cultures as new ideas subvert the old … think of what happened when people discovered the world was not flat or that diseases were caused by germs or, for that matter, when Christianity emerged to supplant older traditions. Such shifts can change whole societies but, on a smaller scale, we too can be shaken when insights or experiences take us out of our usual ways of being and doing. Sometimes to go deeper into our relationship with God, we have to let go of ways of seeing and believing that are no longer authentic or have served their purpose. Are there aspects of your own beliefs and ways of 'doing' faith that need to be let go of so that you can live in more depth and truth? Are you hanging on to them because that's the way it's always been and you've never thought to question them, or because the possibility of change is too frightening?

The footpath brings you to a T-junction at the centre of Tallentire. Turn left and walk through the village for about 20 yards, taking the right-hand turn out of the village and picking up the footpath across fields to Bridekirk.

Alternatively, take a right at the T-junction and follow the road round and southwest to the same village a mile away. Proceed through Bridekirk, and as you exit the village take the left turn towards the A595. This is a very busy road – so proceed carefully – with not much in the way of a footpath at the side, but cross over after a quarter of a mile and there is a minor road to the right. Follow this past Redmain towards Blindcrake, taking the footpath off to your right through fields and towards Gill Wood. Here you will meet another minor road, which cuts through the middle of the wood, where you turn right towards Isel (with the lovely church and yew trees of St Michael and All Angels').

Isel is another name of Brythonic origin, meaning 'low'; you are indeed in a low valley here where Blumer Beck meets the River Derwent. As you walk upstream, this river will be your companion all the way to Crosthwaite, after which it rests in the great lake of Bassenthwaite. Ahead of you and to the south are the Borrowdale Fells, where the river begins its spectacular journey. From this low point in the valley, the hills of Setmurthy stand before you and beyond them the mountains of the Northern Fells. You can stay on the road to St Michael and All Angels' or take a short footpath (where there appears to be a fallen standing stone) through Calfshaw Wood and back to the road.

Reflect upon the low points in your life. What was your experience of the Beloved during those times? And what about during the high points? What helps to call you up from the depths when life is difficult? What grounds you when you are on the heights? It's natural that we should want to avoid the spiritual lows and keep to the highs, but are not both part of the spiritual life? Perhaps the task is to understand and practise equanimity (as in the story of Isa ibn Maryam, Jesus, son of Mary, in part 4 of Coming Home*).*

After passing St Michael and All Angels', follow the road around to the left and continue for a mile towards Long Close Farm (as you leave the road here, the track to the farm and beyond is the footpath), the River Derwent, Buckholme Lonning and Armathwaite Hall. On the left, just before the hall, is a wildlife park. One morning as I walked through the frost I hit upon the incongruity of the sight of a zebra in an English winter landscape.

Have there been times in your life when you have felt out of place, not quite belonging, or a foreigner in your religion? What provoked that feeling? How has it been resolved, if at all? Do you feel completely at home, or are there gritty points of alienation? Are you able to hold these contradictions, and if so how? Is your relationship in the Beloved and with your church, if you have one, the same thing?

After Armathwaite Hall, you reach the B5291. Turn right, and after a 200-yard walk there is a left turn onto the footpath that goes by Cottage Wood and along the northern shore of Bassenthwaite. Stay with this path to Scarness, from where you can follow the curve of the shoreline. If you are lucky, in the summer you may catch a glimpse of an osprey. These magnificent raptors returned to Bassenthwaite in 2001 after almost a century of absence due to persecution. The path then brings you briefly to a minor road, with the great lump of Ullock Pike ahead of you, before turning off rightwards across fields to the wonderfully located St Bega's Church. The church is not one of our Kentigern churches, but is dedicated to St Bega, who gave her name to the town of St Bees on the west coast. Bega was the legendary daughter of an Irish king of the Middle Ages, who fled an arranged marriage, desirous of following the religious life. Landing at what was to become St Bees, she is believed to have founded a religious order. Her cult became widespread in Cumbria.

Many churches have struggled with issues of gender and sexuality down the years, not least through differing views on full equality for women and gay people. What does this mean to you? Are you part of a church that seeks to exclude, or include, treat people as equals, or hold differences? What are the consequences for yourself and the church? How do you hold this balance and possibly conflicting views in your own life? What prayers, and solutions, are needed to foster wholeness, holiness, for your church, whatever your views?

After perhaps visiting the church, continue your walk past Mirehouse, then for another quarter of a mile up to the A591. Cross this (often busy) road here to access a woodland path along the edge. Stay with this route for the next 2 miles along the bottom of Dodd Wood, taking the left-hand fork of the Y-junction at the end of the wood. This minor road is much safer than the A591, and takes you to the village of Applethwaite. You are now walking along the roots of Skiddaw's mountainous bulk to your left. Pass through Applethwaite and stay with the road as it curves south through Ormathwaite and returns to the A591 at a major roundabout; here the A591 and busy A66 meet. Take the path around the roundabout, crossing the A66 (carefully) and exiting to follow the Keswick signs. The road and path towards Keswick crosses a bridge over the disused railway line. After the bridge, turn immediate right down the first street (Vicarage Hill) and follow it for about 200 yards, passing a school on your right, and round to St Kentigern's Church at Crosthwaite. The church is normally open during the day.

At Crosthwaite you have arrived at a location with a specific mention in Jocelin's *Vita*. This is '*Crossfelde*' where, Jocelin says, Kentigern preached to a crowd of 5000, erected a cross and founded a church. The present building is probably the fifth or sixth since that time.

As you enjoy this sacred space and the rich history, perhaps offer prayers of appreciation for a safe journey on the longest single stretch of the pilgrimage. What does it feel like to have reached this far with but one more journey to complete before you reach your starting point? Consider all the stories of our saint and his churches that you have come across on the way. Saints tend to be idealised, put beyond normal human needs and behaviours. But Kentigern, if Jocelin and the old legends are right, has walked this way before you, and with considerably less equipment and opportunities for his comfort and safety. Allow yourself time to reflect upon Kentigern as an earthy, living, breathing human being – just like you. And here, you sit or stand in a place deeply associated with him, his memory and his faith – a place where he stopped to share that faith and inspire others over fourteen centuries ago. He found his path of service – what about you?

As you take time to pray, reflect and meditate in this church and its environs, give thanks for safe passage on the journey thus far. Reflect and journal about your insights, and prepare yourself for the next stage of the pilgrimage.

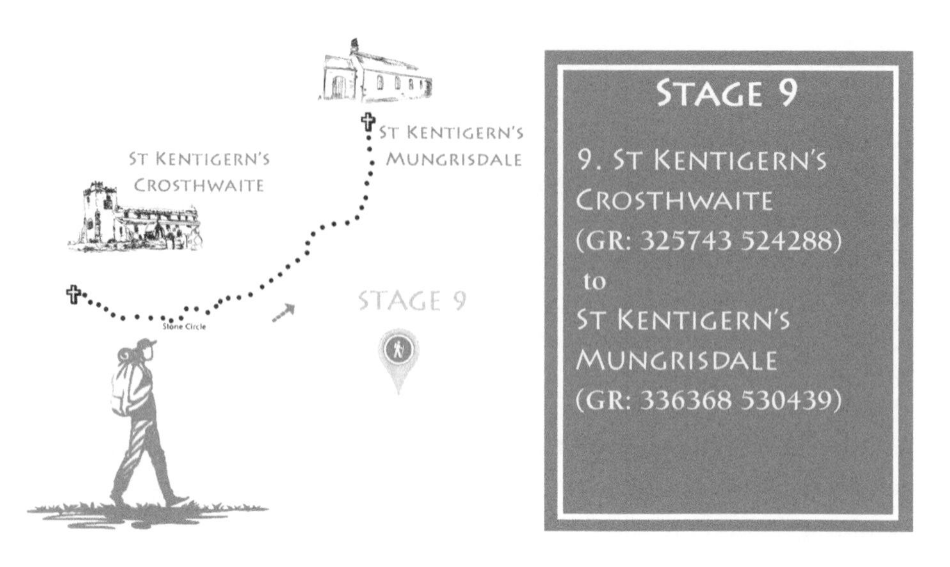

Before you set off, pause in the church and bring the prayerful questions at the bottom of page 99 into your heart and mind. Allow yourself to be receptive to what the Spirit is saying to you.

The last leg of your pilgrimage is before you. Now is a time to take stock and be receptive to what it is the Beloved wants you to pay attention to as you journey towards your starting point, which lies some 11 miles ahead of you. If you have transport, return to the A66 at Crosthwaite and head eastwards for about 9 miles. As you pass the looming presence of Blencathra on your left, there is a turning signposted Mungrisdale and the church is just under 2 miles along this road.

The 12-mile route for walkers takes about 6 hours, depending on your pace, and is well away from the busy A66 for the most part, with some bigger hills this time as you move away from the coastal plain and the river valleys. Once again you will be gifted with wonderful scenery – as indeed you have along the whole of this pilgrimage.

The route from Crosthwaite skirts Keswick. Retrace your steps from St Kentigern's Church, past the school and along Vicarage Hill to the T-junction at the main road, with the roundabout on your left. Cross the main road, turn right and there is a minor road about 100 yards further on. Turn left towards Brundholme, and follow this road for about a mile, passing the sports centre and leisure pool on your right. After about 200 yards past the leisure pool, the road takes a sharp right turn and here you will come to an old railway bridge above it. Bear left just before the bridge and a series of steps will take you up to a foot/cycle path on the disused railway line. Turn left and follow the path. The next bridge you come to, about 250 yards along the path, crosses the River Greta. Stay on the path for almost half a mile and you will approach a road bridge overhead. This is the A5271. Veer to the right before the bridge, off the path, to join this road, then turn right. After 100 yards take the left turn onto the A591 signposted Castlerigg Stone Circle. After 50 yards, turn right along Elventrees Road, also signposted Castlerigg. Follow this minor road steadily uphill for about three quarters of a mile to the stone circle. It is clearly signposted. With this ancient sacred site on your right, there are grand views of the massive bulk of Blencathra (also known as Saddleback) to the left and ahead of you.

It is also possible to walk through Keswick town centre from Crosthwaite, staying with the main road ahead of the church and straight into Keswick, over the bridge over the River Greta and through the town centre along by the park (on your left) to pick up the A5271 heading east out of the town, with a slow uphill plod to the A591. From here follow directions as above to Castlerigg.

Kentigern seems to have made a clean break with the Pagan religion of his ancestors, or at least according to Jocelin. The historical evidence is much less clear-cut and suggests a lot of accommodation and integration took place. And what of your ancestors down the long chain of history that has brought you to this point? How do you honour them? If you hold to a particular religious tradition, how do you keep to that alongside the many different ways of seeing the spiritual life all around you? How do these ancient stones, now largely treated as objects of tourist or archaeological curiosity, speak to you of the long story of humanity and the search for the Beloved? Some people still come to worship here, seeking to revive a religion that was almost lost. The Christian tradition is hardly uniform and has evolved over time. How has your faith evolved? How do you hold both past and present, and possible futures, in your faith and in your relationship with the Beloved? All sorts of reasons have been put forward as to why our ancestors chose this site of Castlerigg: alignment with lunar or solar phases, the procession of the stars, 'earth energies' or mountain alignments. All or none of these may be true, but taking in the panorama around Castlerigg, I have often thought that maybe they just liked the view.

Turn right as you leave the Castlerigg site and the walk continues with the views of Blencathra and its great buttresses to your left. Half a mile after Castlerigg, there is a T-junction; turn right and follow the road round over Naddle Bridge (alternatively, just after Goosewell Farm, cross over a stile on your right and there is a footpath across fields to Naddle Bridge) then straight on past Burns Farm towards the A66. To avoid this busy road (with a cycle track at the side but no paths) take the path on your right before the road. This is the old railway line again. Continue for about a third of a mile up to the road bridge at the B5322. Turn left off the railway path here and cross over the road by the bridge. Follow the path ahead of you through the campsite and on across fields to Mill Bridge.

As you ready to cross the bridge, consider what inner bridges you have crossed. Bridges carry you over difficult terrain; they join opposites together. What opposites have you bridged in your life and on this pilgrimage? What bridge(s) have helped you cross over difficult times, or brought you a sense of unity? Across the tremendous bridge of over 1400 years, does the life and faith of Kentigern still speak to you today?

Cross the river here and follow the footpath on your right alongside the river for a mile. You have now rejoined the River Glenderamackin for this last part of your pilgrimage, the river that was with you at the very beginning in Mungrisdale. Follow the course of the river and enjoy its company before you separate once more at Guardhouse Bridge. You will meet it again in a little while.

From Guardhouse Bridge take the waymarked path across the fields, up the hillside and over the stile to meet the A66 at Scales. Cross the road here and take the minor road at the rear of Scales, known locally as the 'gated road' (no guesses why, as you will soon find out!), and follow it for the next 3 miles along the underbelly of Souther Fell. Enjoy the quietness this road brings as you pass beyond the raucous A66. As you come to the end of this road, on your right is the pinfold, an old sheep-holding space now restored as a small public garden by the villagers.

The space is circular, and you are close now to completing a circular peregrination of the Northern Fells. Rest in the garden momentarily. Where does a circle begin and end? Who and what have you encountered on the way that has challenged or inspired you?

As you walk on into the village of Mungrisdale, cross the bridge over the Glenderamackin and pause: be aware of the river's presence once more.

Cast a twig or pebble into the river: let it symbolically and prayerfully take away something you are ready to let go of. Keep an eye out for another stone or a leaf or other small item to pick up and carry with you as a memento of your pilgrimage, and as a symbol of what you want to take with you on the ongoing circular journey of your life.

Pass through the village; the church is ahead of you. Now is the time to stop, rest and reflect. The pilgrimage, at least the travelling of it, is complete, although it is in the nature of pilgrimage that its impact may be felt for the rest of your life, subtly, and sometimes not so subtly, reverberating with a sudden remembrance or insight or new awareness of integration. As a result of this journey, perhaps you have become more aware that all of life has been speaking to you, all the encounters, nature and buildings – there is nowhere that God is not – all has been reaching out to draw you ever closer to Home.

Keep your journals; share your experiences with a Soul Friend or your Soul Community. End the pilgrimage with a time of prayer in St Kentigern's Church, Mungrisdale. Be thankful for your safe return and for all the gifts along the way. Ask of the Beloved:

Beloved God,
now that I am here at the completion of this pilgrimage,
and as I ready myself to move on to the next stage of my life:
What is it You want me to receive?
What is it You want me to know?
What is it You want me to let go of?
What is it You want me to do?

THE KENTIGERN WAY

Wild Goose Publications, the publishing house of the Iona Community established in the Celtic Christian tradition of Saint Columba, produces books, e-books, CDs and digital downloads on:

- holistic spirituality
- social justice
- political and peace issues
- healing
- innovative approaches to worship
- song in worship, including the work of the Wild Goose Resource Group
- material for meditation and reflection

For more information:

Wild Goose Publications
The Iona Community
21 Carlton Court, Glasgow, G5 9JP, UK

Tel. +44 (0)141 429 7281
e-mail: admin@ionabooks.com

or visit our website at
www.ionabooks.com
for details of all our products and online sales